ALANA VALENTINE is a Sydney-based playwright. In 2013 *Tinderbox* was produced by Tredwood Productions at Darlinghurst Theatre 19, and *Comin' Home Soon* at the Leider Theatre, Goulburn. In 2012 *Tarantula* was produced at the King Street Theatre and *Grounded* was presented by Tantrum/**atyp** at the Civic in Newcastle and at the Wharf in Sydney. In October 2012 Alana was presented with the prestigious 5th STAGE International Playwrighting Award for *Ear to the Edge of Time*. She was also nominated for a fifth time for the 2012 Griffin Award for *Lavender Bay*. *Cyberbile*, commissioned by PLC Sydney, was first presented December 2011. Two of her community-sourced plays are on the NSW Higher School Certificate Drama syllabus (*Run Rabbit Run* and *Parramatta Girls*). Her Queensland Premier's Literary Award nominated play *Head Full of Love* opened in 2012 at the QTC after a premiere season in Darwin, Alice Springs and Cairns and also aired on ABC Radio National. Alana's documentary-style project-making has seen her involved with multi-disciplinary works which involve visual art, creating an installation for the Goulburn Regional Art Gallery of a joint work by Goulburn Correctional Centre inmates and children of inmates which companioned the aforementioned stage play. Alana also conceived an origami ribbon fish sculpture and storytelling event called *Swimming Upstream* for ASCA's (Adults Surviving Child Abuse) Blue Ribbon Day associated events. In August 2013 her play *Dead Man Brake* will be presented at Merrigong Theatre in Wollongong.

Scott Gelzinnis as Jim, Matt Baird as Jack and Dean Blackford as James in the 2012 Tantrum Theatre production of Grounded in Newcastle. (Photo: Justine Potter)

CYBERBILE
&
GROUNDED

ALANA VALENTINE

CURRENCY PRESS
SYDNEY

CURRENCY PLAYS

First published in 2013
by Currency Press Pty Ltd,
PO Box 2287, Strawberry Hills, NSW, 2012, Australia
enquiries@currency.com.au
www.currency.com.au

Copyright: *Cyberbile* Foreword © Greg Friend, 2013; *Cyberbile* © Alana Valentine, 2011, 2013; *Grounded* Introduction © Fraser Corfield, 2013; *Grounded* © Alana Valentine, 2012, 2013.

COPYING FOR EDUCATIONAL PURPOSES

The Australian *Copyright Act 1968* (Act) allows a maximum of one chapter or 10% of this book, whichever is the greater, to be copied by any educational institution for its educational purposes provided that that educational institution (or the body that administers it) has given a remuneration notice to Copyright Agency Limited (CAL) under the Act.

For details of the CAL licence for educational institutions contact CAL, Level 15, 233 Castlereagh Street, Sydney, NSW, 2000. Tel: within Australia 1800 066 844 toll free; outside Australia +61 2 9394 7600; Fax: +61 2 9394 7601; Email: info@copyright.com.au

COPYING FOR OTHER PURPOSES

Except as permitted under the Act, for example a fair dealing for the purposes of study, research, criticism or review, no part of this book may be reproduced, stored in a retrieval system, or transmitted in any form or by any means without prior written permission. All enquiries should be made to the publisher at the address above.

Any performance or public reading of *Cyberbile* or *Grounded* is forbidden unless a licence has been received from the author or the author's agent. The purchase of this book in no way gives the purchaser the right to perform the plays in public, whether by means of a staged production or a reading. All applications for public performance should be addressed to RGM Artist Group, PO Box 128, Surry Hills NSW 2010. Tel: +61 2 9281 3911; Fax: +61 2 9281 4705; Email: info@rgm.com.au

The moral right of the author has been asserted.

NATIONAL LIBRARY OF AUSTRALIA CIP DATA

Author: Valentine, Alana, 1961– author.
Title: Cyberbile & Grounded / Alana Valentine.
ISBN: 9780868199849 (paperback)
Target Audience: For secondary school age.
Subject: Australian drama—21st century.
Dewey Number: A822.3

Typeset by Dean Nottle for Currency Press.
Front cover design by Heath Killen.
Cover design by Katy Wall for Currency Press.
Front cover shows Jemima Webber as Farrah in *Grounded* (photo Justine Potter). Back cover shows Sasha Ognjanova as Community Figure in the 2011 PLC Sydney production of *Cyberbile* at Audrey Keown Theatre, Sydney (photo Leonard Elliot).

Cyberbile & Grounded was created with assistance from the Commonwealth Government through the Australia Council, its arts funding and advisory body.

Contents

CYBERBILE	1
Foreword	
Greg Friend	3
GROUNDED	49
Introduction	
Fraser Corfield	51

Currency Press acknowledges the Traditional Owners of the Country on which we live and work. We pay our respects to all Aboriginal and Torres Strait Islander Elders, past and present.

Sophia Mobbs as Oriana and Kassandra Kashian as Celine in the 2011 PLC production of CYBERBILE *at the Audrey Keown Theatre, Sydney.*
(Photo: Leo Elliot)

CYBERBILE

Natalie Cox as Dancing Nightmare, Sophia Mobbs as Oriana, Rachel Simpson as Dancing Nightmare and Katrina Sioufi as Dancing Nightmare in the 2011 PLC production of CYBERBILE *at the Audrey Keown Theatre, Sydney. (Photo: Leonard Elliot)*

FOREWORD

Drama is a powerful tool to educate and inform its audience. It can open deep wounds, awaken suppressed emotions and explore ways of healing or changing lives.

In 2011, one of the Drama staff at Presbyterian Ladies' College, Sydney, Joanna Golotta, wanted her senior Drama club to create their own piece of theatre.

The senior students had been studying verbatim theatre as part of their final HSC course and had embraced the concept of real testimony driving a theatrical performance, and this was the form they wanted to write in. Initial discussions were based around topic areas—what could a group of 15- to 17-year-olds explore with a certain level of knowledge and understanding? The answer was found in our first meeting.

Cyber-bullying. It's everywhere. It creeps into our kids' bedrooms late at night and infests social media outlets for all the world to see. Everyone can be reached and no-one with a mobile or an email address, a tumblr account or Facebook is immune to this dreadful plague.

Our school had recently conducted a survey into this epidemic and whilst our results returned a really positive analysis there was still evidence that some among our school community were engaging in this terrible form of bullying. Further research by our group uncovered the fact that it's a massive issue in schools right across Australia. One school had attributed three suicides in 18 months to online bullying. The statistics were horrifying.

And so we created an anonymous survey and handed it to every girl in Years 7–12. Over 700 surveys came back. Most of them were what we as a school would want to read. Students had not experienced online bullying, or they knew of someone who had but hadn't been part of it themselves. However, a small proportion uncovered a terrible world out there where some hid behind anonymity and made other students' lives a living hell. I should point out that some of the stories were from students' pasts in other schools which is why they made the change to PLC. In saying that, there was enough evidence that cyber-bullying was also prevalent amongst our students.

The survey also allowed students the option of revealing their identity so that they could be interviewed further. Thirty-four girls came forward wanting to tell their story. Over the course of three weeks we interviewed all 34 students. Some of the stories were very hard to sit through and we were so appreciative of the girls having the courage to come forward and share their experiences.

After typing out the transcripts of the interviews and sifting through the 700 surveys, we sat down and started to collate the material into a theatrical piece. Verbatim theatre is not only about the words on the page, it is about the dramatic structure and the 'reveals' to the audience. It didn't take us long before we realised that we needed help. Professional help.

Joanna had been to one of Alana Valentine's workshops earlier in the year and Alana's beautifully written *Parramatta Girls* was one of the texts we studied in Year 12. I wrote to Alana on a whim asking if she would be interested in being involved in our project. To my utter surprise and relief she agreed to meet with us and consider our proposal. The rest is history, contained in the pages of the script you now have.

Alana took our material away and came back three weeks later with a structure that allowed the content to come to life on stage. In the style of 'massaged verbatim' Alana took the story of one of our students and created the character of Oriana. The play follows her journey as a victim of cyber-bullying and her determination to stand up to this vile form of intimidation.

The process to get to a final script was a long one and such an incredible experience for our students. Alana was so generous with her time, often coming in to workshop the scenes and shuffle the monologues to ensure maximum impact. Our students were living any actor's ideal dream—to be able to work alongside one of Australia's great playwrights and to see firsthand how a script is developed from concept to reality.

The production was co-directed by Joanna Golotta and myself in December 2011. The audience response was tremendous and it started a dialogue around the school that we believe has made a positive impact on our students.

Joanna's vision and determination, coupled with Alana's skill and creativity is a wonderful example of the strength of Drama as a subject in schools. It exemplifies how professionals and students can collaborate in the creative process and PLC Sydney is eternally grateful to Alana for her vision and courage. Currency Press also deserves kudos for agreeing to publish this important piece of Australian theatre.

Cyber-bullying will be hard to fully eradicate in society. However, through plays such as *Cyberbile*, the hope is that this cowardly form of bullying will be greatly diminished and its victims will find the courage to stand up for themselves, and those who know bullies in their social groups will expose them for what they are.

Greg Friend

Greg Friend is Head of Drama at PLC Sydney.

Sinead O'Farrell as Oriana, Petronie Lufu, Courtney Bullock, Timothy Drummond, Thomas Quinn, James Lynch and Bianca Jones in the 2012 Nepean Creative and Performing Arts High School production of CYBERBILE *at the Q Theatre, Penrith. (Photo: Matthew Sullivan)*

Cyberbile was first produced by Presbyterian Ladies' College, Sydney, at the Audrey Keown Theatre, Croydon, on 1 December 2011, with the following cast:

ORIANA	Sophia Mobbs
CELINE	Kassandra Kashian
TERRI	Ruby Kerr
FIGURES	Charlotte Rowse, Georgina Chard, Helen Mchugh, Natalie Cox, Elloisa Candi, Simone Ireland, Alya Higgins, Annie Watson, Rosie Bailey, Rachel Simpson, Katrina Sioufi, Sasha Ognjanova, Anastasia Balis, Lily Murphy, Elise Harrison, Georgia Dodd, Jessica Blake, Natassia Chrysanthos

Directors, Greg Friend, Joanna Golotta
Lighting Designer, Alex Grierson
Sound Technician, Jared Lattouf

CHARACTERS

FIGURES 1–12 These include cyberbullies, cybervictims, parents and teachers. When the figures reappear in the script they are never the same character they were previously so, in truth, the figures could be played by many more than 12 performers, at the director's discretion, or the 12 specified. Similarly the figures are often non-gender specific and may be changed by small alteration of pronouns, though with some of the figures this may not be appropriate.

CELINE, 16

ORIANA, 16

TERRI, 16, may be played by a female or male performer

SET

The work should be played on a set which allows the individual worlds of the students, teachers and parents to be realised, as well as the 'office' where Celine, Oriana and Terri are conducting their research. The theatricalised 'dream' sequences with matadors and bulls should be as colourful and dynamic as the director cares to make them.

NOTE

The author would like to thank Miss Joanna Golotta and Mr Gregory Friend from PLC Sydney for commissioning this work and also for providing such rich verbatim source material for me to draw and build upon from interviews with their students, teachers and parents. Although this material is substantially drawn from transcripts, it has been 'massaged' and dramatised by me in significant ways so that it does not accord precisely with any single source and should be regarded as documentary-inspired fiction.

AV

SCENE ONE

FIGURE 1: I was… I guess I was sitting at my computer and I was replying to an email and I just typed one word that was stronger than I usually use and the word was 'slut' and I just typed it and it felt good to use a stronger word and I sent it off and nothing happened and it sort of just went from there. I would describe it that… as I started using stronger and more forceful words on the screen… like I found this total word for it which is vitriol and that's what it's like… like by shooting this vit into the email then the less there was in me. Like it was as if the second I saw this nasty shit appear on the screen then I had ejected something out of my own body and I have to tell you that felt good. And so I found myself actually looking for situations where I could like overreact and just really spill that bile out of me. Mostly anonymously. I guess it's not so different to wanting to march in the streets or dye your hair green, it's just about being really verbally rebellious yeah? Like everyone knows you're not supposed to but it honestly feels really good. Just to shoot off stuff like that. Like it's venom. And it's just in you and then it's just… out of you.

FIGURE 2: Yeah, I've really liked it when Formspring has got particular to certain schools and to people you know because I like to watch the reaction. Like even if people are really upset it's not like I'm heartless, it's just that I'm more kind of absorbed by watching their reaction than caring about what they're going through. Which sounds harsh but I don't mean it like that. I mean it like… it's like being in a story or a show or something and you're the one pulling the strings. Like you can't pretend that that sort of power is not cool. It's way cool. You write something and then in the real world, in people you see, it's affected them. Really big-time. And you're probably thinking that I'm some sort of psycho but I'm not. I just did it once… like unintentionally did it once, wrote something that really upset someone and I felt bad about that but then, I dunno, I just stopped feeling bad and just started being fascinated by what a big reaction it was and so I wanted to do it again. It gave me something to look forward to, which I know is pretty lame. But it did. I bet I'm gonna get in trouble for admitting all of this.

FIGURE 3: This whole thing about cyberbullying… I am just so over it because… because I like to use the internet to say what I think and if that's gonna be labelled bullying then I'm up for that. I mean you hear girls say that someone online told them that they were fat or ugly and they're really devastated by that and I mean honestly I just have no tolerance for that kind of indulged, overprotected princess behaviour. If it takes little old me to give them a reality check then so be it. Some of these girls are such wimps, it's like they sue the school for breaking a fingernail you know. 'Oooh, someone said I looked bad in that dress last night. I'm being cyberbullied.' Get over yourselves. I have written that to girls online. I tell them how lame they are. Because they need to get real about how privileged they are and how trivial their concerns are. I bully girls online because they need to stop being such a pack of wimps. And if they don't want to know the truth then they shouldn't go online and look into their profile. You know?

SCENE TWO

ORIANA: Hello and welcome to the world of social networking and online bulling. My name is Oriana Matthews and I am a student at Silver Wattle High. Earlier this year we conducted a survey about students experiences of cyber friendships and these are the results.

CELINE: No, don't say 'these are the results'.

ORIANA: But they are the results.

CELINE: Yeah, but you sound like you're announcing the Eurovision Song Contest voting scores. [*In an accent*] 'I am Inge from Sveden and here are the results of the Svedish jury.'

ORIANA: That's racist.

CELINE: Everyone makes fun of Eurovision.

ORIANA: Well, I don't think it's funny.

CELINE: Fine.

ORIANA: Should I explain about how we conducted one-on-one interviews with students from Year 7 through to Year 12?

CELINE: You mean girl-on-girl interviews.

ORIANA: What's wrong with you today?

CELINE: Nothing. I'm always like this.

ORIANA: So just quit it.

CELINE: Who's a cranky pants, Spongebob Squarepants today?

ORIANA: I'm not.
CELINE: Is this stuff getting to you?
ORIANA: What?
CELINE: 'The results from the Svedish jury'?
ORIANA: No. I think that stuff that came in from the bullies is kind of gold.
CELINE: It is, isn't it?
ORIANA: No-one was owning up to it in the surveys.
CELINE: 'Maybe I might have bullied once but I didn't realise I was doing it.' Yeah sure, and I didn't realise my pants were on fire.
ORIANA: You've got a fixation on the word pants today.
CELINE: Have not.
ORIANA: Have so.
CELINE: Speaking of bullies.
ORIANA: Yeah well, setting up the site where they could send stuff anonymously has really worked.
CELINE: So has anything else come in?
ORIANA: Sort of.
CELINE: How can something sort of come in?

   ORIANA *hands her a piece of paper.*

ORIANA: But it's nothing.
CELINE: [*reading*] 'Oriana Matthews you dumb slut, stop working on this cyber shit project or we will stop you because you are sick trash. You're nothing but a fake whore who thinks that you are better than other people.'
ORIANA: So they're testing me.
CELINE: Sounds like they're threatening you.
ORIANA: It's nothing.
CELINE: Don't you think we should tell Miss Pardelote?
ORIANA: No way.
CELINE: Why not?
ORIANA: Because… I don't want them to close down the project.
CELINE: They won't. They'll just trace them.
ORIANA: And then that becomes the story of this project. That I ran to the teachers as soon as it started getting interesting.
CELINE: You don't have to say that.

ORIANA: It's verbatim. It has to be authentic.
CELINE: Not totally.
ORIANA: Yes, totally.
CELINE: Fine.
ORIANA: If they do it again we'll talk about what to do.
CELINE: Meanwhile the researcher becomes the research?
ORIANA: Well, sometimes the journalist becomes the story.

SCENE THREE

FIGURE 4: I think you can hear why I get bullied. It's pretty different. I guess it's just that to me it's really normal because I've always had it. So I'm used to it. I even got offered a voice-over job on a film once when I was thirteen. I didn't get it but they did a test and everything and the director said he really loved it, you know, my voice. Some people think it makes me sound masculine I suppose. But it's not masculine it's just deep. Plenty of women have deep voices and husky voices. Heaps. I even read how actresses sometimes do stuff to make their voices deep and husky, like smoke, I guess. I was a premmie baby, premature, and that's how it happened because there were all these tubes down my throat in those early weeks. I don't call it damaged because I don't think of it as a negative. Anyway there was this one girl, she was sort of a friend of mine for a while and then she just turned really nasty, started to ignore me and stuff. Like I'd say hello and she'd just ignore me and so I knew something was wrong and then I started getting these really heavy emails, saying I was basically a man and I was probably deformed and saying how she couldn't stand to be around the sound of my voice because it was like a sleazy old man in a pub and all this stuff. And I didn't tell anyone about it for a long while, even though I knew you're supposed to. I guess because I was deep down really ashamed of myself so it's not like it felt justified… more just that I didn't know if people would think it was fair enough because my voice is so deep. I'm not explaining it properly but since I've got older I know that people can hurt you most with the things that you dislike about yourself the most. When we did *Othello* for drama I realised that. Which is damned sophisticated don't you think? Even if I do say so myself. Anyway… the thing you doubt about yourself is the place where they can really get in. Big-time.

FIGURE 5: We have these school trips where you go overnight on excursions and that's where this particular bullying started. You have to share and I was sharing with this girl who was in a form lower than me and anyway she saw that I was reading a Mills & Boon. At first she was just razzing me as if it was a joke you know swooning about and making up really cheesy lines as if she was the handsome heroine. And then at night she would wake me up and start reading out bits of the book to me. Like in the middle of the night and I was in a deep sleep. It was really weird and then when we got back from the trip I kept getting these emails with quotes from various Mills & Boon in them and no name signed but of course I knew it was her. And the trouble with it is that she could have just said that the whole thing was a joke between friends and that's what she told me she would say. Even when I told her that I didn't like it… because then she started posting stuff about how I had never had a boyfriend and I never would because I was really frigid and because I have never had a boyfriend everyone believed her and there was nothing I could do. And I was in real trouble there for a while. Sorry. It obviously still gets to me even though in my head I'm totally over it. Sorry. A couple of nights I spent the whole night crying so I'd get to school with really red eyes. And I got really paranoid imagining that people thought I was crying because I couldn't get a boyfriend but it was really because of this girl who just wouldn't leave it alone. She was a real bitch. We never resolved it really she just stopped which was good. I still don't have a boyfriend but that's okay.

FIGURE 6: Last year I was away for the whole term in Germany, going to school there and when I was over there I was checking my Formspring and there were lots of comments saying, 'don't come back, you don't belong at Silver Wattle High', and stuff like that, but luckily I am a strong person and I really didn't care. I find it kind of amusing how people were bothered enough to do that and yeah, these people tended to write as if they were the whole perspective of the year while I knew I had friends here. Some of the messages would say, like, 'no-one at Silver Wattle High likes you', 'don't come home', and it was stupid because I obviously know I have friends because I was in contact with people and they couldn't wait until I got back. So it was yeah, kind of stupid. And the other main thing has been with me and my boyfriend 'cause he's a bit older and people he is friends with have come on to my Formspring and said, 'what are you gonna do with him?' and things like that and then go onto his and say that 'going out with a 14-year-old I've lost a lot of respect for you', and things like that. He's 18 and he is still in school and he's been my best friend for ages. We're actually family friends so we go to family dinners and things, it's not a big deal. We're not planning to do anything big of course. But you still get comments like, 'oh, if age is just a number then jail is just a room', and it's like well that's just stupid, he's not going to jail. It's not like he's a big predator or anything like that—it's really stupid but, um, we both find it really amusing actually.

SCENE FOUR

ORIANA *enters with two figures either side of her. Both are wearing horned 'bull' heads which might be masks or* papier-maché *prosthetics. They complete the actions as described in the poem—winding a sheet around her and spinning her in it, dragging her to and fro like a cocooned silkworm, then pasting words and letters onto her, not necessarily coherent but perhaps with asterisks and stars. There also might be an 'el bulli' chorus of smaller bull figures who dance or otherwise move during these dream sequences.*

ORIANA: I had a dream that was not all a dream
and in it I was stalked by horned creatures
'el bulli'
and my sheets were wound around me
tight as the night
wrapped like a cocoon
like a worm
and their weapons
were not knives
were not swords
but felt the same

their weapons were words
used commonly
brute
raw
without beauty or clarity
only short
vulgar words
to seal my misery
words like blades
their edges sharp and razor-like.
Awake, my helpers and come, my friends
for I am needled with cruel jokes
and my courage is flowing away from me
my confidence seeps out of me, like blood.

> *There might be a dance sequence here with music and choreographed 'binding' and unbinding of* ORIANA. *Finally she is left in a heap on the floor.*

CELINE: Oriana?

ORIANA: What?

CELINE: Are you okay?

ORIANA: I feel really tired. Do you get days like that when you just feel so tired?

CELINE: Maybe you should go home.

ORIANA: I want to collate those new replies that have come in.

CELINE: So you've seen it?

ORIANA: Seen what?

CELINE: Do me a favour and delete your Formspring account.

ORIANA: Why? What's on it?

CELINE: It's just some weirdo. You don't want to see it.

ORIANA: Tell me.

> CELINE *goes to the computer and brings it up.*

I have herpes? But I don't have herpes.

CELINE: They're gonna make it your thing.

ORIANA: But it's not true.

CELINE: Watch it become true.

ORIANA: It can't become true.

CELINE: Of course not.

ORIANA: So what do I do?

CELINE: It sort of doesn't matter what way you respond to it, people will assume that you're hiding something. Like with a case like this, if you say no people are going to think 'oh, she's lying' and if you joke about it they're going to say 'she's hiding something' and if you get angry they're going to say 'you're trying to hide the truth'. So it's one of those things you just can't win. On the other hand, you can't let it go unchallenged because then everyone will just think it's true.

ORIANA: They've posted the date I went to the doctor as evidence.

CELINE: So they've hacked into your email.

ORIANA: Are you joking?

CELINE: Did you confirm the doctor's appointment on email?

ORIANA: On sms. Oh, and there was an email.

CELINE: So.

ORIANA: But it wasn't even for that. It was a flu vaccine.

CELINE: They've got it.

ORIANA: What is this? An episode of 'SVU'?

CELINE: Now we report it.

ORIANA: No.

CELINE: Yeah, we do.

ORIANA: I want to see what happens with it.

CELINE: What happens is that everything turns to rat slime.

ORIANA: I'm fine. I don't care.

CELINE: Someone has hacked your email.

ORIANA: So I won't use my email.

CELINE: Oriana. I'm serious. You have to report this.

ORIANA: Celine. I'm seriously fine with this. What do I care about some anonymous lie? But I am interested in how other people react. This is more gold, for the project, you know.

CELINE: So you're asking for it.

ORIANA: I am not.

CELINE: Listen to you, you're almost pleased this is happening now. While you're doing this project.

ORIANA: Yeah, but I'm in control of it.

CELINE: They're saying you've got herpes.

ORIANA: What if I can work out who it is?
CELINE: Why would you want to do that?
ORIANA: To find out what people really think of me. I'm curious.
CELINE: But you don't even know if it's someone you know.
ORIANA: It must be for them to know my name. They still have to type in my name to make it come up. So they must know me.
CELINE: So that's worse. Some sicko you know is doing this. Saying stuff that they won't even say to your face. Maybe they don't even mean it, they just want to see how you react.
ORIANA: So I'll show them. If this survey has taught me anything it's that you've got to stand up to them. Period. And if I can find out who they are they'll get exposed. In this project. Big-time humiliation. Stick that in your herpes cream, Nurse Ratchett.

SCENE FIVE

FIGURE 7: So I'm a young woman. Obviously I'm a young woman and here's the scariest thing about what goes on. I think it's the same as what has always gone on but because it's in print on the net it just seems uglier. But that's not what I mean by the scariest thing. The scariest thing is this—you scratch just under the surface of what boys are thinking and you get this massive, massive dose of misogyny. Right there. They call you slut, they call you whore. They brutally rate you on your physical attributes like a meat market. And if they talk about sex they make really crude comments about how much you, for instance, moved or not. Comments about how you smell, comments about various bodily fluids and whether there is too much of them, if you know what I mean. And this comes close to the scary thing for me, like, I just can't believe that this is not what young men have always talked about you know and that's the scariest thing for me. Because you want to believe that only a few boys are nasty freaks but with the root-rater sites and all of that you see that it's more that the nice guys are the exception and I don't know if I can explain this but for me as a young woman that really puts me off boys. Like I'm not saying that I'm going to turn into a big lezzo or anything but it still puts me off trusting boys. Not just for sex either. More just… for any reason. Like I wonder if we are the first generation where the ugliness of adolescent men and the ruthlessness of young women is really right there en masse in print. It's just the sheer organisational hatred of women that really shocks you. Am I making any sense? You kind of sense that it is there but in our generation it's right there. You know. And a lot of the nasty comments are about girls and their appearance, seriously. Boys get it too but for girls it's just totally there. And you hear about newsreaders and other women in the public, what's it called, public face, public eye, they get the most hideous feedback on especially their appearance. It just… freaks me out, I mean is all society like that. Is there this deep-seated hatred of women like everywhere?

SCENE SIX

ORIANA *is hanging in a 'web' of telephone cables and wires onstage. She is caught there like a fly in a spider's web.*

ORIANA: I had a dream that was not all a dream
and in it I was trapped in a web
not of my own making
and lines of lies were wound around me
indelible as the past
forever available
and this weapon was not poison
was not acid
but felt the same
their weapon was rumour
and lies
forever suspended on servers
cruel
wrong
without the possibility of compassion or forgiveness.
Awake, my courage and come, my faith
for lies are written on my body
and my sanity is flowing away from me
my hope leaks out of me, like hot tears.

    She is crying in a pile on the floor when CELINE *enters.*

CELINE: What's happened?
ORIANA: It's nothing.

CELINE: It's not nothing.
ORIANA: It is. I'm just being lame.
CELINE: What's happened?
ORIANA: I can't…

> *She is having trouble breathing she is so distressed. After a moment she recovers herself.*

CELINE: I'll be you.
ORIANA: Okay.
CELINE: I'll be you.
ORIANA: Okay.
CELINE: Where did I go?
ORIANA: Party.
CELINE: The party at Emmaline's?
ORIANA: Why weren't you there?
CELINE: I wasn't invited.
ORIANA: You be me.
CELINE: I'll be you, invited to a party at Emmaline's.
ORIANA: Yes.
CELINE: And who are you?
ORIANA: I'm this guy.

> *She bursts into tears again.*

CELINE: What guy?
ORIANA: Just a guy.
CELINE: The guy from the beach.

> ORIANA *nods.*

He was there?

> ORIANA *nods.*

What happened?

ORIANA: You know I had seen him that time at the beach and he bought me that can of Coke.
CELINE: You liked him.
ORIANA: I thought he was okay.
CELINE: You liked him.
ORIANA: Maybe I did.
CELINE: What happened?

ORIANA: Well, I was just getting, I dunno, getting something from the kitchen and he came in and he just said to me… [*She starts crying.*] He asked me if I… you know…

CELINE: What?

ORIANA: I can't.

CELINE: I'll be you.

ORIANA: He told me he liked me but he needed to know if I really had herpes.

CELINE: He did not.

ORIANA: He did. Which means he's been looking at my Formspring profile.

CELINE: So you just said, 'no of course I don't'.

ORIANA: That is what I said.

CELINE: And that's it.

ORIANA: That's it?

CELINE: I mean. That's what you said to him?

ORIANA: No, I looked at him and I was so shocked that I just went really red in the face and I shook my head but he just stood there and then he started looking around and he said, 'yeah, whatever', and then he just left me standing there.

CELINE: You won't be so shocked next time.

ORIANA: What?

CELINE: I mean next time you see him.

ORIANA: Celine. That information is up there forever.

CELINE: You can delete it.

ORIANA: And what about the next party I go to? Or don't, more's the likelihood. How do I know how many people have seen it?

CELINE: You'll be laughing it off by then.

ORIANA: I won't.

CELINE: I told you to report it.

ORIANA: Do you think it was him?

CELINE: What?

ORIANA: Do you think he was the one who put it up that I had herpes and he did that at the party to see whether I had been affected by it?

CELINE: I thought you liked him.

ORIANA: He reckons I've got herpes!

CELINE: But was he… like was he really asking or was he doing it deliberately to upset you?

ORIANA: How should I know?

CELINE: Well, was he like laughing or was he sincere?

ORIANA: I can't remember. It's a blur.

CELINE: So what did you do then?

ORIANA: I got maggoted.

CELINE: Why?

ORIANA: Because it's a really sensible thing to do when you're upset.

CELINE: It's not like you.

ORIANA: No, and I don't have herpes either. But apparently that is now my profile.

CELINE: It's not.

ORIANA: I'm never going to another party again.

CELINE: You will.

ORIANA: What would you know, you weren't even invited.

Pause.

CELINE: I'll upload whatever's come in.

ORIANA: Okay.

CELINE: You should go home.

ORIANA: You think it will be alright?

CELINE: I'm sure it will.

ORIANA: Okay. [*Pause.*] Sorry.

CELINE: Don't worry about it.

ORIANA: Celine.

CELINE: Don't worry about it.

> ORIANA *gives her a kiss on the cheek and exits.* CELINE *continues to enter information into the computer.*

SCENE SEVEN

FIGURE 8: Yeah, I am a bully but I'm like the Dexter of bullies. You know 'Dexter', the TV show. There's this TV show about this guy who is a serial killer but he's a really good serial killer, you know. He is. He only kills people who are already murderers, or child molesters. So he's kind of like an avenging angel. Well, I'm an avenging bully for my friend. She had sex with this guy and then he blogged about it in explicit detail, the scum, and so I started to bully him, like for her. I put stuff up about how I had slept with him too and he had a really small you know what and he was really hopeless and he cried and stuff. I'm sure it wouldn't have affected him one bit but I still did it and it felt good to at least put words up against him. The scum. He totally deserved it.

FIGURE 9: My mum has been teaching me to drive and you know, all my life when we are in the traffic my mum yells at the other drivers. Not bad stuff, well yeah, swear words and stuff but lots of sarcasm you know, 'oh, that was a really smart thing to do dickhead', or 'get back in your own lane you imbecile', stuff like that. Sometimes quite loud and sometimes she holds up her little finger like in those ads about speeding and I asked her about it once and she said that in the city the traffic is so fast-paced and aggressive that it's almost just a way to psych herself into the role. Like she said she's just playing a role, like working herself up into a state where you can like push in where you need to and cross across where you need to. Because let's face it you can't be all polite and get around. You just can't. So… what's that long story about, girl? Well, just like my mum's traffic aggro has never turned into road rage I think most cyberbullying is kind of the same, it's just this kind of role you play to be part of the online community… you give a little bit of attitude and stuff but that doesn't mean that you necessarily want to turn into a full-blown bully. Like you're going to encounter bad drivers and aggressive drivers and you need to give back as good as you get but really it's just part of driving and you shouldn't get too hung up about it. Same with online chat—you're going to get a bit of attitude and a bit of aggro but just blow it off and keep going. If it turns into road rage and you're getting out of your car with a tyre iron to smash up someone's car then it's a problem but if it's just low-level aggro I don't think it's a problem.

SCENE EIGHT

ORIANA *stands in the centre of the stage. As each of the 'el bulli' characters speak they throw some kind of sticky substance at her.*

FIGURE 1: Oriana Matthews is a just a tease, bro, she can't make up her mind, she's not worth it and you should no way consider asking her out.

FIGURE 2: How do you think she got herpes, mate? She goes with the chattest guys. You're way above her.

FIGURE 3: Yeah, who wants to poke some herpes-affected hole, boy.

FIGURE 4: I would. Just to get a photo you know.

FIGURE 5: Ask her to send you a photo of herself. Ask her for topless first and see if she will.

FIGURE 6: She will, man, she's a total slag that one. Make sure you pretend to be nice though. Suck it up so you can suck it up, if you know what I mean.

Makes a slurping noise.

FIGURE 7: Best time to do it is right now. She wants to get back in with everyone so for sure she will send it.

FIGURE 8: Go for the full naked view.

FIGURE 9: But get it on your phone so we can all see it.

FIGURE 10: What if she gets the cops involved?

FIGURE 11: They never do. Posh school like hers will handle it internally. They never get the cops involved. Even if they find you, which they won't, most you will get is a slap on the wrist.

FIGURE 12: And you get the big O nude on the net.

FIGURE 1: You gotta get her drunk, man.

FIGURE 2: At a party, go up and ask her if she's got herpes.

FIGURE 3: That'll make her reach for the bottle.

FIGURE 4: Then when she's smashed you gotta film it.

FIGURE 5: Topless.

FIGURE 6: Humping.

FIGURE 7: All the bases and a home run.

FIGURE 8: But finger her first, man, or you'll get her herpes on your own hot dog.

FIGURE 9: And if she turns you down we'll say she's a lez.

FIGURE 12: We'll say she's a desperate lez even if she does it.

FIGURE 1: She deserves it man because she is a lez.

FIGURE 2: She got the herpes from a lez gang bang.

FIGURE 3: Didn't you know lez's all work the Cross?

FIGURE 4: That's 'cause they're all drug scum, man.

FIGURE 5: That's how she got the herp. From her little lez scum mates in the Cross.

FIGURE 6: But you gotta get the bang on film.

> ORIANA *collapses into a heap on the floor.*

ORIANA: I had a dream that was not all a dream
and in it I was slicked with substances
like oil
like garbage
and the casual nastiness of it
stripped away my innocence
and tore away my trust
and no amount of tears could wash away the contempt
and I itched and I scratched and I wiped
at the muck
at the stink of careless bile
and I lifted my head to the heavens and cried.
Why is this happening to me?
What have I ever done to deserve this?
All I did was try to talk about what's happening
and I thought I could take it.
Come back my ignorance, return my joy.
For I have stripped back the mask of adolescence
and my sanity is shrivelling on the vine.
My grip on reality is loosened beyond all saving.

SCENE NINE

FIGURE 10: I don't really want to identify myself because I don't want to do a one-on-one interview. Like I'm fine with being gay and most of my friends are fine with it, what am I saying, all of my friends are fine with it. But being gay is always going to be the thing that gets some bullies going. I dunno, maybe I'm being negative but sometimes I think you're just never going to stop it. Things are much better. And people tell you that all the time. How much better it is. I know it is. The thing is it's not just the external bullies that get you, though they're pretty bad. If you get unlucky enough to be targeted you can get a really hard time for a while. The trouble with coming out is that it's always hard on you not because it's seen as bad or wrong but just because it can take a long time to work out if your feelings are real and whether you can trust them. So coming out to yourself is hard enough without being outed or accused of it by nasties online. It's never not going to be hard in a way because it's always going to be outside the norm. And all the schools can do is not condemn it or problematise it or such. My parents know and they are okay with it. 'Cause there's not even the thing anymore that you're going to be unhappy or not have children or such. It's just always going to be different to them I guess. I wouldn't go so far as to say no parent wants to have a gay child because even that's really changed. But I dunno what I'm trying to say. Yes, you get cyberbullied for being gay, yes you get actual bullied, yes you bully yourself. Yes it's more complex than outright abuse, it's like when you choose to come out, about how there's always a pause and people say 'oh, well that's okay' as if you need their approval or something… when I say that people say, 'well, what would you want them to say?' 'Cool, you can help me with my formal dress or something', 'cause everyone knows gays are good at fashion but what do they know lesbians are good at? Maybe fixing cars. I dunno. That's stupid. But there's not a thing you can say—like Australians like to joke to show that they're cool but there's not a dyke stereotype joke. Maybe they could say, 'Great, can you give my boyfriend some tips on how to be a good kisser because everyone knows dykes are good kissers'. Ha!

FIGURE 11: There's this site—bebo—where you could give people love and you'd look at it and there would be 'oh my gosh, I've got almost no love, I'm so unpopular da da da da dahh.' Then other people would make fake accounts and give themself love. I dunno if it was insecurity but I remember people saying 'I have two accounts so I can give myself love so it looks like I have more love'. It sounds pathetic but people see if you have tons of love and think you're popular and even if they don't believe it, you want them to believe that rather than not.

SCENE TEN

CELINE: Who are you?

TERRI: I'm Terri, who are you?

CELINE: I'm Celine. Where's Oriana?

TERRI: She's sick.

CELINE: What's wrong with her?

TERRI: I dunno. She's just at home. Miss Pardelote asked me to work on some of the transcribing and stuff for the project.

CELINE: Right.

TERRI: Did you know she's been getting some really dodgy stuff?

CELINE: It's just part of the project, isn't it?

TERRI: Well, maybe it is but it's still pretty foul.

CELINE: She's been asking bullies to write in.

TERRI: Yeah to talk about why they bully. But not to actually bully her.

CELINE: What do you mean?

TERRI: There's stuff here about her having herpes and stuff.

CELINE: How did you access her email?

TERRI: Miss Pardelote gave me her password.

CELINE: That's an invasion of privacy.

TERRI: Not on a school project it's not. Anyway, I reported it to Miss Pardelote and they're investigating it.

CELINE: What?

TERRI: Yeah, she said they might be able to trace where the emails came from.

CELINE: But that will blow the whole project and all the work Oriana has been doing.

TERRI: Why?

CELINE: Because the bullies will all stop writing in. Now we won't get anything from them because they'll all be scared they're going to get traced.

TERRI: So they should get traced.

CELINE: We said they wouldn't.

TERRI: Too bad.

CELINE: You shouldn't have reported that stuff without Oriana's permission.

TERRI: Someone had to.

CELINE: What?

TERRI: Well, you were obviously not being a friend to her.
CELINE: You don't know anything, slag.
TERRI: Don't call me slag. Who do you think you are?
CELINE: Oriana is my best friend.
TERRI: Then you should have told her to report this before it got out of hand.
CELINE: I did tell her to report it but she wanted to keep going with it as part of the project.
TERRI: Some friend.
CELINE: I told her to report it.
TERRI: Maybe that's why she didn't listen to you. Because you're not really her friend.
CELINE: I don't have to listen to this from you. This is our project and I am going to tell Miss Pardelote we don't want you on it.
TERRI: And you're gonna be in trouble when I tell Miss Pardelote that you knew about this bullying and did nothing about it.
CELINE: We'll see when Oriana gets back.
TERRI: Maybe she's not coming back.
CELINE: She is so.
TERRI: Then where is she?
CELINE: Anyone can get sick.
TERRI: Especially when they've got herpes.
CELINE: Why are you being so nasty?
TERRI: You were the one who called me slag.
CELINE: I shouldn't have said that. I'm sorry.
TERRI: You just don't want me to tell Miss Pardelote you said it.

Pause.

CELINE: Why do you want to take Oriana's project away from her?
TERRI: I don't.
CELINE: Then why are you here?
TERRI: Well, maybe because I've been bullied, der.
CELINE: Oh.
TERRI: Oh, she finally gets it.
CELINE: Alright you don't have to be so rude.
TERRI: Well, neither do you.

Pause.

CELINE: What happened to you?

TERRI: Why should I tell you?

CELINE: Look. I really am sorry. Okay.

TERRI: Okay, well… I used to have a really nice group of friends and I was really happy until Year 6. Then there was this group of people who for some reason didn't like me. They stole my friends, they told them to go against me, they spread rumours about me, so I had no friends and for about a whole year they did stuff to me.

CELINE: Like what?

TERRI: The stole things from me, like they stole things from my pencil case, and so I made sure I didn't bring my favourite things to school because I was worried they would take them. They'd write in my books, they'd hide my bag at lunch and recess and at the time I didn't really know it was bullying because no-one really told me about what bullying was, I just accepted that 'oh well, this is what my life is, it just has to be like this'. And I didn't tell my parents anything… because… I don't know, I didn't really think things could change, I just had to accept that my life was sad. My parents were really worried, they noticed. They said, 'why are you always sad, you never smile anymore, you never seem to enjoy things'. Outside of school I had some friends, but they never really knew anything about my school life. I went to Chinese school every Saturday, and that was like the only time I was really happy because they liked me. I used to be quite smart, like I used to win awards and stuff and then afterwards I did really badly and my parents were really sad for me. They used to buy me books. Because I really liked reading, I used it as an escape and I started writing.

CELINE: And did they use online too?

TERRI: I gave one of my friends my email account password and she sent people rude emails. And the really bad person, the person who stole my friend, she went into my friend's email account and started sending things to me, so I thought it was my good friend saying those bad words. So I thought no-one liked me. Which was true, no-one liked me. And then I joined bebo because people were like, 'Oh, why don't you have a bebo account?' So I joined and then not long after they made a bebo hate group. It was like a group that was dedicated to hating me and they took random pictures of me at school that I didn't know about and then put wired captions and then add it to the group. And then these girls, they started doing graffiti and when I found out I was 'no that's wrong' so I told one of my close friends or who I thought was my close friend. I was like 'maybe we should tell the teacher about this because they are trying to find out who graffitied the school hall, I know it's them because I overheard them talking about it and they were full bragging about how cool they are doing graffiti', and then, um, my friend was like 'oh good, do that'. But before I could she told the bad people and they came up and ganged up on me and said 'oh, you wanna tell the teacher, we'll make the whole school hate you if you do that'. I was really scared because no-one supported me and I didn't know what was right or wrong anymore. People told me I was wrong and I didn't have the confidence, I wasn't strong enough to believe that I was right.

CELINE: So how did you get away from them?

TERRI: I had to leave. I had to leave that school. [*Pause*.] And that's why I told you 'bout this stuff on here. Because maybe you say she was dealing with it as part of the project but maybe she's just saying that. Because I didn't know what to do, I didn't even know what it was.

SCENE ELEVEN

FIGURE 12: I get bullied because I'm a Christian. Stuff like 'if you were a Christian you wouldn't do that'. Sort of holding me to a higher standard or something that they're not even prepared to hold themselves to. But they justify it by saying 'well, I don't say I'm a Christian so I don't have to be perfect'. Which is really stupid because I'm not saying I'm perfect. I don't even know why I believe, but I do. I was hoping it might help me and it sort of does. But I'm still going to... you know... um... I guess you might say I'm going to give in. Um. There's this person who is bullying me at the moment and, look, you can say what you like about faith. Some people have power and they can make your life miserable. And I just don't have what it takes to stand up to them right now. Like everyone's always making out how you have to be a hero and how your faith can help you to stand up. But you also don't. You can just do as you're told. You can and you can just believe that there's no shame in that. If I don't resist they'll just move on, you know. I'm just so scared and [*crying*] I just want them to stop hassling me. I'll just do what I'm told and be a bit more secret about my faith. What's so wrong with that? Why does everyone want me to be such a hero? I'm not, alright. I'm just not. Stop expecting me to be the big hero. That's why I believe in what I do, you know. Because I know I'm not strong enough on my own. Not now I'm not. But one day I will be. One day I'll find that strength. Just… just… not right now.

FIGURE 1: Okay when the first person said 'there is no climate change' they were laughed at but now we have to give them a hearing. Well, here I go with this. There is no cyberbullying epidemic. It's a helicopter parent, baby-boomer wowserism. It's schools having to exist in a highly litigious, overheated duty-of-care-gone-crazy environment. It is. People always cite the kids who have killed themselves from cyberbullying. I mean, please. I'm not saying it's not bad, I'm just saying it's the serious exception. Cyberbullying is just one more way for parents and teachers to gate the freedom that teenagers now have on the internet. Seriously. And it's no different to tabloid television going to some beach party in Thailand and using scare tactics about how unregulated it is. It's wowserism. Pure and simple. And considering how many drugs and drink and wild parties these parents did when they were young it's just one hundred percent overprotection. Suddenly parents are shocked by how cruel their children can be online. Wake up. Children are the most cruel because they see the world in black and white and if you give them their dinner, screaming obscenities at the television yourself, what do you expect them to do? Think back to some of the things you did and said as a teenager. Let your children learn that life is unfair, for goodness sake, or they're soon going to find it out the hard way when they go out into the big wide world. Everyone doesn't get an equal chance at life, yes it's a bummer but that's how it is. The world loves clever young men above just about anything else, clever young women can do well for themselves but they're still going to be judged for their looks and they can still never become spiritual leaders or captains of industry or even leaders in our democracy unless they are very, very, very tough. Nothing has really changed and it's the same in our part of the world.

SCENE TWELVE

ORIANA is sitting on the floor. She is surrounded by piles of paper and in front of her is a shredder. She sits and shreds page after page of paper in a kind of zombie state.

CELINE: Oriana?
ORIANA: Hey.
CELINE: Hey. Whatcha doin'?
ORIANA: Nothin' much.
CELINE: What's that you're shredding?
ORIANA: Just… words.
CELINE: Why'd you do that?
ORIANA: What?
CELINE: You've printed out all the bullying stuff that was sent to you.
ORIANA: If I can chew them up and then spit them out then they're nothing, right? Then they're just nothing.
CELINE: Sure.

ORIANA shreds another one.

They said you were sick.
ORIANA: I'm just tired. I've been really tired.
CELINE: Just like from the flu or something?
ORIANA: No, not flu. Just… I dunno… just tired of everything, you know. And a bit teary.
CELINE: Are you okay?
ORIANA: Yeah, I just need to sleep at the moment. Just sleep, you know.
CELINE: You've got to snap out of it, Oriana.
ORIANA: I'm fine. Just a bit tired.
CELINE: You're depressed.
ORIANA: Not really. Maybe a little bit.
CELINE: There's a girl who's working on the project. She reported the bullying to Miss Pardelote.
ORIANA: Yeah, I know. They rang Dad.
CELINE: So what are they doing about it?
ORIANA: I think that they're going to try and trace it.
CELINE: They might not be able to.
ORIANA: Whatever.

CELINE: So… are you coming back to school?
ORIANA: Yeah. Soon.
CELINE: And are you coming back on the project?
ORIANA: I don't think so.
CELINE: Why not?
ORIANA: I dunno. Maybe I can't handle it.
CELINE: But you can.
ORIANA: Yeah, I think I can but maybe I can't.
CELINE: Who says you can't?
ORIANA: I dunno.
CELINE: What's happened to you, Oriana? You don't let stuff like this get to you.
ORIANA: No, it's not that.
CELINE: Then what else is it?
ORIANA: I dunno. I just don't want to go out at the moment.
CELINE: Because you think people are going to think you have herpes?
ORIANA: Maybe.
CELINE: Most people will have just forgotten that.
ORIANA: Yeah.
CELINE: You know how this works, there's always someone new to be picked on. You're yesterday's news, girl.
ORIANA: Yeah. I know.
CELINE: Seriously. I've never seen you like this.
ORIANA: I'm fine. Really. I just don't feel like… I mean… things don't interest me like they used to… it all just seems really futile, you know… like even school and everything.
CELINE: Everything what?
ORIANA: Like the future, you know? What's the point?
CELINE: You should see someone.
ORIANA: Yeah, I think Dad's gonna take me to someone. Like a counsellor or so.
CELINE: You've got to snap out of it, Oriana or they'll put you on… I dunno… pills or something. Anti-depressants which make you really dopey.
ORIANA: I just pretend to take them.
CELINE: What?
ORIANA: They've put me on them already but I spit them out.

CELINE: Why?

ORIANA: I don't need them.

CELINE: Oriana. I don't know what to say to you… you just seem totally different and I can't believe it's because of some bullshit online, you know. You know it's just… nothing.

ORIANA: I know.

CELINE: You don't.

ORIANA: I do. And if I just chew them up and spit them out that will be the end of them.

> ORIANA *puts another page through the shredder.*
>
> CELINE *watches her, still concerned, then exits.*

SCENE THIRTEEN

FIGURE 2: My daughter started cyberbullying because she couldn't handle a situation with a girl at school. The other girl started it but it was my daughter who retaliated. And it was my daughter at the end of the day who got into trouble for doing it. The other child walked out of it scot-free but I don't have a problem with that. She was doing verbal stuff and my daughter was putting it on the net. Friends of mine said that if they were in my situation as a parent that they wouldn't have exposed their child at school. Had I done that, had I covered up for her, I believe that I would have a more conniving child doing worse things to kids now. I think that the earlier we deal with the signs, the earlier we get there, the better. Because children don't just turn up at sixteen as bullies, they start somewhere and I think it's when they're in Year 7 and conflict arises and they don't know how to handle it except by hitting back on the net. I always, when I want to talk to my daughter and make sure she understands, I hold both her hands and look into her eyes, because when you're holding somebody's hands they have to look into your eyes. She took both my hands and I knew straight away what she was going to say to me. A lot of parents think that if they hide it it will be fine but actually what they are doing is harming their child. It was dealt with very privately by the school and now my daughter has been a captain, she is respected in class and she is liked by the teachers. I think people are afraid of it being made public and being labelled and that shouldn't happen either.

FIGURE 3: Children who come from a very strict household basically get punished for doing things at home and so they have to have an outlet so they come to school and misbehave at school. The kids that have a more free environment at home tend to be the ones that are better behaved. That's why I let my kids jump on my furniture. Because when I go somewhere I expect them not to jump on other people's furniture. The kids that come to my house I can generally tell what type of households they come from because if they come and jump on my furniture I know they come from a strict household and if they are well-behaved they come from a relaxed household. So I think that, um, kids that go to school that misbehave at school don't have that outlet at home. I think that both those things tie up with bullying... if you are too strict with a child there is no outlet for them and they have to do it somewhere. They come and pick on kids at school because at home they are raised very strictly.

SCENE FOURTEEN

TERRI: They've traced the bully.
CELINE: Oh?
TERRI: It's a made-up account.
CELINE: I thought it would be.
TERRI: Why?
CELINE: I dunno. Just because that's the gutless way these people work.
TERRI: Have you ever bullied anyone online?
CELINE: Me?
TERRI: Yeah.
CELINE: I guess I might have. I mean... I've written things that were a joke and my friends know it's a joke because they know how I talk... you know?
TERRI: But to someone outside it wouldn't be?
CELINE: To someone outside they might think it's abuse, but it was a joke.
TERRI: Ever bullied anyone anonymously?
CELINE: I dunno. I guess so. Probably everyone has.
TERRI: Why did you?
CELINE: I dunno.

TERRI: 'Cause they can't trace the original bully but they can trace a whole lot of people who joined in.
CELINE: What do you mean?
TERRI: I mean since that first thing...
CELINE: About the herpes?
TERRI: Yeah, once that went up a whole lot of people just like went for her as well.
CELINE: She didn't tell me that.
ORIANA: Because I wanted to know.

 ORIANA *has entered, unseen.*

CELINE: Oriana, you're back.
ORIANA: I'm back.
CELINE: Are you okay now?
ORIANA: Who knows?
CELINE: You look good.
ORIANA: I heard they traced the thing.
CELINE: But not the who.
TERRI: What did you want to know?
CELINE: This is Terri.
TERRI: Hi, Oriana. What did you want to know?
ORIANA: Two people can do exactly the same thing or wear exactly the same thing and one of them everyone will notice them and praise them and the other will either just be ignored or there'll be some—I dunno—some thing that never makes them popular or never makes them... fit.
TERRI: Why is that?
ORIANA: That's what I wanted to know.
CELINE: It's just—the luck of the draw.
TERRI: What draw?
CELINE: How do I know?
ORIANA: Like in last year's Year 12, Tanya Van Mar used to wear her hair in funny creations, buns and plaits on the side and all sorts of structured dos, you know, and then at the school farewell there was a character in the thing—in the mock-up—that had crazy hair and everyone knew it was Tanya Van Mar and she like got to be friends with Anita Ross and met all her model family and stuff.

CELINE: Yeah?

ORIANA: And Grier Wolseley did exactly the same thing with her hair and everyone said she was just a weirdo.

CELINE: It wasn't as good, what she did.

ORIANA: But it was just as original. Maybe more original.

CELINE: But when Tanya Van Mar did it it was cool.

TERRI: But why?

CELINE: I don't know.

ORIANA: Like… is it part of our animal brain or something?

CELINE: Maybe.

ORIANA: But it's true, isn't it. It's not so much what you do but who it is that's doing it.

CELINE: I guess.

TERRI: But then how do you ever become one of the cool people?

CELINE: Why are you asking me?

TERRI: So does that mean, if I'm a picked-on person, that I can change schools and change like everything but eventually people will like… start to pick on me again?

CELINE: Not necessarily.

ORIANA: But probably.

CELINE: Don't say that.

ORIANA: That's why people say why does this always happen to me. Because it does. It only does happen to some people more than others.

CELINE: So they bring it on themselves? So are they doing something?

ORIANA: Not doing something but maybe sending out some signal.

CELINE: That's paranoid.

ORIANA: Well, that's what I wanted to find out. But instead I became one of the…

TERRI: Damned.

They laugh.

Yeah. Well, I reckon old Mr Squarepants can get stuffed.

ORIANA: Who?

TERRI: The hotmail address was squarepants@hotmail.com.

ORIANA *turns and looks at* CELINE.

ORIANA: Was it you?

CELINE: What?

ORIANA: It was, wasn't it?
CELINE: How can you even say that?
TERRI: What?
ORIANA: You were calling me that.
CELINE: It's a character. It's…
ORIANA: Why?
CELINE: Oriana, that's just crazy.
TERRI: What is?
ORIANA: Why?
CELINE: I think you'd better go back home. I really don't think you're as over this as you think.
ORIANA: What? It started off as a joke maybe? Thought you'd just help along with the project?
CELINE: I don't have to listen to this from you. I thought you were my friend.
TERRI: Will one of you please tell me what is going on?
ORIANA: Tell her.
CELINE: She's somehow got it into her crazy brain that I am Squarepants.
ORIANA: Because she is.
CELINE: Tell Miss Pardelote that I'm off this project.
ORIANA: I know it's you.
CELINE: You really have lost it. Totally lost it.

CELINE *exits*.

TERRI: Why do you think it would be her?
ORIANA: Well, who else would it be?
TERRI: It could be anyone. It could be me.
ORIANA: Why would you do that?
TERRI: Why would Celine?
ORIANA: So I'd need her to… I dunno… console me. Support me. Since it happened we've got a lot closer… maybe she wanted that.
TERRI: That's a pretty viral thing to do to… I dunno… prop up your friendship.
ORIANA: If it was her it would explain a lot.
TERRI: And if it's not you've just wrongly accused your friend.
ORIANA: Maybe.

SCENE FIFTEEN

FIGURE 4: It shocked me a lot. My child had been an angel up to then and the shame was it was literally in front of my eyes… it was terrible. Having to face that school appearance was a shocking trauma for me. I was ready to nail her up to the door but, um, I also realised that children are going to be children. The reality of it was that part of me did no longer trust her and even now I still always have the slightest suspicion when there is a problem. So, it shocked me beyond words. But I had no problem admitting it to the school that my child had admitted it to me or forcing my child to make that telephone call to that other little girl. I had no problem doing that. I knew that the next six months was going to be tough for me as a mother. Nothing flowed on into the playground though. I think the other teachers asked the other parents to keep it quiet and that's exactly what happened. Now that was a very useful thing to do actually because it allows you to move on, you know what I mean, it means that, ah, you don't have to wake up and think I need to get out of this environment, I need to move schools. I think handling it in quite a private way it helped a lot. It doesn't have to be done publicly, it can be recognised that it is just part of growing up and part of being a child. I think a lot of parents think that it could never be their child. My child is a very good child, she is very thoughtful and wants to please other kids. I think the law says it's actually up to seven or eight that children actually don't always know if something is right or wrong. So you know children do a lot of things that they are not sure is right at that age because they haven't realised that teasing is not quite right, lying is not quite right. As parents it is our role to start to see these things first. I remember going through my kid's bag and if she even had a pen that didn't belong to her I would make her take it back. I think there are a lot of parents that would think 'oh, it's only a pen, it doesn't matter', but it does. Now even if my child finds something on the street and says 'oh, I found five cents', I say 'no, put it back'. Do you know what I mean? That five cents belongs to somebody, so my child automatically knows now 'oh, that belongs to somebody. I have picked it up by accident I have to put it back tomorrow.' I think all of these things… I think as a parent we have to be diligent about all of these tiny little things and yet I had ignored it at times which lead to problems with my daughter. My daughter was complaining about this little girl and I ignored it. I thought it was little-girl stuff and I basically didn't even bother to give her decent answers so she decided she was going to take the solutions in her own hands. If I had listened to her as a parent perhaps it wouldn't of happened.

FIGURE 5: As a parent I'm not very computer savvy, I'm just a user. I've learnt a few things like, um, if my... I know how to go into the history and see what my daughter has looked up. She knows that I know how to do that. I say to her 'you have to behave appropriately online because anything you do online can be tracked by anybody, anybody anywhere can find actually what you have looked at'. And to prove it to her one day I sat her down and showed her the history and she saw that I could look it up. That's keeping her in line.

FIGURE 6: Don't hide your child. If you need to expose your child to authorities like the teachers, the teachers were wonderful at the time. I had just bought my daughter's Christmas present that cost about $500 and I wanted to take it back and they said 'don't take it back, separate the two of them'. My child did not get into trouble at school probably because of the way I handled it myself, I don't know, age, I don't know, but I got a lot of support from the teachers in terms of how to handle it and not to be too harsh with my child. In terms in what happens at home my child now does not have availability to the computer. It's the ramification that is she aware of.

SCENE SIXTEEN

All the FIGURES *are splendidly dressed as matadors, in wonderful hats and coats.*

ORIANA: I had a dream that was not all a dream
and in it there appeared a host of matadors
their red rags waving
bright as balloons
to bring on the enemy
they ducked
they weaved

their bodies turning on muscled torsos
arms and rib cages lifted into their finery
a prance of power
a dance of death and blood
a ritual slaying
and in my dream I ran among the toreadors
begging them to spare the brute
pleading for the life of the beast
who turned then and gored me through.
Awake my senses and come intuitions
for I am wounded by my own blindness
my lifeforce pools and eddies down my arms
toward the dust that is the earth.

> *When* CELINE *enters,* ORIANA *has blood pouring down her arms onto the ground. Both her arms are covered in blood.*

CELINE: What have you done?
ORIANA: I was a toreador. In my dream.
CELINE: Oriana?
ORIANA: They were killing the bull.
CELINE: I'm going to call an ambulance.
ORIANA: No.

> ORIANA *struggles and grabs* CELINE*'s phone. She also wipes blood on* CELINE.

CELINE: What are you doing?
ORIANA: Tell me.
CELINE: Oriana. You've got to let me call.
ORIANA: Tell me why.
CELINE: Let me call and I'll tell you.
ORIANA: No. Tell me first.
CELINE: Alright.
ORIANA: Why did you start it?
CELINE: I didn't. It wasn't me.
ORIANA: Then who was it.
CELINE: I don't know. We may never know.
ORIANA: Why couldn't you say it to my face? Why couldn't you just say it to me?

CELINE: How about something just to stop the bleeding.

> CELINE: *takes something and wraps it around* ORIANA*'s hands.*

ORIANA: It really wasn't you?
CELINE: No.
ORIANA: But I know it was.
CELINE: Why would I do that?
ORIANA: I don't know. Maybe you don't know yourself.
CELINE: No.
ORIANA: Maybe it was just… to help make the surveys interesting. You couldn't have known that all the others would come on and keep it going.
CELINE: Whoever did it couldn't have known that.
ORIANA: Was it you?
CELINE: No.
ORIANA: It was though, wasn't it?

Pause.

CELINE: I can't find where you've… I can't find any wound…
ORIANA: [*screaming*] Tell me!
CELINE: Oriana, calm down.
ORIANA: Tell me!
CELINE: Alright.
ORIANA: Alright it was you?
CELINE: Yes.
ORIANA: It was you who wrote that I had herpes.
CELINE: It was a joke.
ORIANA: A joke?
CELINE: It was so far-fetched. I thought it would just make you shake your head.
ORIANA: And what? Confide in my friend. Have a laugh about it together?
CELINE: Yeah.
ORIANA: This is the truth now?
CELINE: Yes.
ORIANA: YOU LYING BITCH!
CELINE: Let me call the ambulance.
ORIANA: I'm going to get you expelled for this.

CELINE: Alright. Anything you want. Anything you want. Only let me call the ambulance.
ORIANA: What ambulance? It's paint.
CELINE: What?
ORIANA: Paint. It's red paint. Fake blood. Get it?
CELINE: You're crazy.
ORIANA: I'm crazy why? Because I fooled you? Because I pretended to be something I'm not. I'd have thought you could pick a fake. Being one yourself.
CELINE: Is it really paint?
ORIANA: It's food colouring.
CELINE: Why would you do that?
ORIANA: What, you thought I would try to kill myself? Over some vindictive bitch like you. I wouldn't bother. People shouldn't kill themselves in response to some low-life like you. They should cover themselves in red paint and get their own back.
CELINE: Oriana, this is so totally extreme.
ORIANA: To make you confess.
CELINE: You frightened me half to death, you bitch.
ORIANA: You're the bitch. You're the lying, deceiving piece of shit that I thought was my friend.
CELINE: You wanted me to do it.
ORIANA: I did not, you sick hag.
CELINE: You would never have told me anything. You would hardly have even looked at me as a friend if I hadn't. And yes, I liked that you depended on me, I liked that you trusted me and relied on me. I liked it. So what? So freakin' what?
ORIANA: I am so going to get you expelled.
CELINE: Get away from me.

    CELINE *exits.* ORIANA *screams after her.*

ORIANA: Yes, walk out! Walk out and pretend that's the end of it! People think I've got a venereal disease because of you, so now you can never leave! Congratulations! My so-called schoolfriend is going to be with me for the rest of my life! Every time someone googles my name it will be you, not me that they're seeing!

SCENE SEVENTEEN

FIGURE 7: Because I'm an English teacher I'm actually interested in the language of the online world. I mean, there are basically now three registers of language. Formal, colloquial and cyberspeak which is mostly slang and abbreviations. OMG. LOL. Smiley face. Sad face. And somehow I think that young people think that by abbreviating words they have less power. That if you say someone is f, star, star, k'd that somehow you diminish the impact of that. And then if everyone is using those abbreviated forms of abuse and normalising it that people can just flip it off and be kind of teflon-coated. I worry that by diminishing the words we use and reducing it all down to a kind of code speak that we are in fact diminishing the breadth and the depth with which we can think about things. The complexity with which we can think about things. I mean, I'm not advocating that people on social networks should all write in rhyming couplets or sonnets but I do wonder about... I dunno... the lack of poetry in cyberspace. And somehow... I may be drawing a bit of a long bow here but go with me... somehow when you reduce language to a whole lot of abbreviations and you simplify language down into words of one syllable or less somehow that contributes to a brutalising of our feelings and our emotions and our spirits. Language is such a wonderful treasure trove—because words contain the struggle to be understood in a complex way. People have invented words for ideas and feelings and things that wouldn't in a way exist unless we had a word for them. People are always saying these days that they can't put their feelings into words and sometimes I wonder if it's less about there not being any words for their feelings than they just don't know the words or having taken the trouble to seek them out. But I'm an English teacher so of course I'd say that. What I'm really trying to say is that ugliness of behaviour is somehow, sometimes reflected in ugliness of expression. And I'm going to tie myself in knots because some people who speak simply can be wonderful, kind people and some people who speak in a sophisticated manner can be horrible, pompous and nasty. Actually I don't know what I'm trying to say except that a lot of cyberbulling is really crass and vulgar and diminishes us as human beings. We're better than that and young people are better than that. Young people contain such beauty and such hope and such brilliance of possibility and as an English teacher I want to fill them up with words that can… I dunno… make all that just shine out of them.

SCENE EIGHTEEN

ORIANA *is sitting, reading a book.*

TERRI: Whatcha doin'?
ORIANA: I'm practising my trapezoid handstands.
TERRI: There's no need for sarcasm.
ORIANA: Well, I think I'm pretty clearly reading a book.
TERRI: I don't want you to bite my head off.
ORIANA: Maybe better not to speak to me then.
TERRI: You hanging out by yourself a lot these days?
ORIANA: What of it?
TERRI: Nothing. I just thought you might want some company.
ORIANA: If I do, it won't be you.

Pause.

TERRI: Don't let her do that.
ORIANA: Here we go.
TERRI: Don't let her make a bitch out of you.
ORIANA: Maybe I always was.

Pause.

TERRI: You still think she did it?
ORIANA: She told me she did.
TERRI: She reckons that she said that to make you call the ambulance.
ORIANA: I know what she reckons.
TERRI: Anyway. I wanted to give you this.
ORIANA: What is it?

She hands her a matador gold shoulder epaulet.

TERRI: One of the outcomes of the cyberbullying project is this thing called Matador Mondays where people can come and talk to someone about a bullying issue they might be dealing with. And if you're the designated counseling matador you get to wear the shoulder piece. If it takes off we could have people all over the school wearing them just one day a month.

ORIANA: Who's going to go to that?

TERRI: Maybe no-one.

ORIANA: No-one is right.

TERRI: But even if they don't come and report it, it will keep the issue on people's radar and you never know, somebody might just reach out or a bully might think twice before they go for it.

ORIANA: Expel Celine. That will send the bullies a message.

TERRI: Will you wear it?

ORIANA: No, Terri, I won't. I've asked you to go away. I've asked you nicely and I've been rude and now I'm going to be very rude. Leave me alone and don't push this matador bullshit on me. There is no justice, all the teachers pretend like it can all be dealt with privately and we can all make it up and work it out and be friends. But I'm the one who has to live with what people think of me being out there, forever.

TERRI: I know.

ORIANA: Are they saying you have diseases? Are they?

TERRI: No.

ORIANA: Then you don't know and you get stuffed with your crappy little matador bullshit.

TERRI: Don't speak to me like that.

Pause.

ORIANA: I'm sorry. But you pushed me.

TERRI: I didn't push you. I asked you to be part of something positive. You've got no right to abuse me like that.

ORIANA: You're right.

TERRI: I know I am.

ORIANA: I'm sorry.

TERRI: You can't speak to people like that. Not on the net and not in person.

ORIANA: I said I was sorry.

TERRI: You're so busy moping about what Celine did or didn't do. Face it, you'll never know.

ORIANA: I do know. And I know that she's going to get away with it.

TERRI: So what?

ORIANA: So what? That's not justice, that's not fair. The world is rooted.

TERRI: And what are you going to do? Just curl up in a little ball and whine about it?

Pause.

ORIANA: Now who's being a bitch?
TERRI: Not really.
ORIANA: Yeah.
TERRI: Some friendships come with a bit of tough love.
ORIANA: I'll say. [*Pause.*] I just want her to be punished.
TERRI: But they can't prove it so she can't be punished.
ORIANA: But that's not good enough.
TERRI: No, it's not. But it's how it is.
ORIANA: Well, I don't accept that.
TERRI: Alright. Stew away then.

TERRI begins to leave.

ORIANA: Wait.
TERRI: No, I don't think I will.
ORIANA: Wait.
TERRI: Why should I?
ORIANA: Because. [*Pause.*] Who thought of the title Matador Mondays?
TERRI: Me. Why?
ORIANA: It's lame.
TERRI: Lame?
ORIANA: Cheesy lame.
TERRI: The little kids will like it.
ORIANA: Maybe.
TERRI: Well, can you think of something better?
ORIANA: Of course I can.
TERRI: What?
ORIANA: Toreador Tuesdays?
TERRI: Oh yes, I can immediately see the superiority in that.
ORIANA: What'd I tell you?
TERRI: Toreador Tuesdays. So much bolder, so much easier to remember.
ORIANA: Thank you.
TERRI: Yeah, right. [*Pause.*] Want to come and talk to Miss Pardelote about it?
ORIANA: Sure. We'll say it was my idea.
TERRI: Of course.
ORIANA: Alright then.
TERRI: Lead on, 'el toro'.

SCENE NINETEEN

FIGURE 8: My dad says that if I can learn the value of the cyberworld, the value of personal learning networks and social networks and if I can learn to use them, well, I've got a chance of winning. He used to say that this was all particularly difficult in an all-girls environment because girls deal with things differently. 'Girls can be incredible bitches,' he'd say, 'if you don't mind me saying so.' He told me... 'If you have an argument with somebody in the class I want you to go outside with them and I want you to beat up on each other because that's what boys do and they end up as friends rather than let any issues linger and fester.' But now that I've shown him stuff on the sites, the stuff that the boys say to the girls and the boys say to each other, he doesn't say that anymore. When I showed it to him he shook his head and said 'it's a different world, it's such a different world', and he, and I was really shocked, he looked right at me and said, 'I don't know how to help you with this. I don't know how to help you but I don't want to fail you.' And I said, 'Dad, you don't need to solve it for me', and that was all I said but now, every now and then he'll ask me how I'm going and I mean honestly I wouldn't tell him everything because some of it would just freak him out. But I know, I do know, that, if it ever got bad or even if I thought I was handling it but could tell that I wasn't, I would tell him. I would go to him. Because he's seen what it is and he wouldn't be all shocked now. He told me that he wasn't part of the cool group at his school, he said that he was a dag and when he goes to school reunions, not that I've ever known him to go, but he said whenever he goes he still kind of gets left out and that's by the mean kids. He said the mean kids never go away you just get better at not caring what they think. But he wouldn't get involved in any problem I had unless I asked him to. He says, 'at the end of the day you're teenagers and that's how teenagers roll'. 'It's like giving you dating advice,' he said, 'at the end of the day you have to figure out for yourself what's right or wrong. And find out who your real friends are and who'll stick by you.' So... yeah... I don't care if he thinks he's still a bit of a dag... he is a total dag, you know... but he's also a teeny bit... only the teenest little bit... but still a very little bit cool.

THE END

Clockwise from top: Siobhan Caulfield as Chloe, and Scott Gelzinnis, Naomi Dingle, Dean Blackford, Tamara Gazzard, India Wilson and Emily Daly as Figures in the 2012 Tantrum Theatre production of Grounded *in Newcastle. (Photo: Justine Potter)*

GROUNDED

Tamara Gazzard as Mother, Emily Daly as Mother, Jemima Webber as Farrah and Naomi Dingle as Mother in the 2012 Tantrum Theatre production of Grounded *in Newcastle. (Photo: Justine Potter)*

INTRODUCTION

Grounded was developed as a co-commission between Tantrum Theatre from Newcastle and the Sydney-based national youth theatre company, Australian Theatre for Young People (**atyp**). As the Artistic Director of **atyp** I was involved in the development of the script as dramaturge from the initial idea to the opening night.

It's interesting to recall that the first discussions about this work in March 2010 weren't with Alana, but with Tantrum Theatre's then Artistic Director Brendan O'Connell. Both companies were committed to the development of new Australian plays written specifically for young actors. We had talked about the prospect of working together on a piece that could engage an audience in Sydney, but would be specific to the tone and culture of Newcastle. The aim was to tell a unique Newcastle story that everyone would be able to relate to. We also discussed the prospect of working with a leading Australian playwright likely to develop a script that would go on to be published and presented by schools and youth theatres around the country. Days later Brendan forwarded the proposal from Alana Valentine for the commission that went on to become *Grounded*.

Looking at the original synopsis proposed by Alana, it is remarkably similar to what became the play. So often with projects of this type the final script can bear little semblance to the initial discussions and project ideas. The most notable change was the name. *Grounded* was initially proposed as *Tanker Town*, a catchy title that speaks to the armada of bulk carriers that tend to be anchored just out to sea beyond the busy port on any given day.

But that title only lasted as long as Alana's first research trip to Newcastle. She quickly informed us that the name had to be changed because they were not 'tankers', they are bulk carriers moving coal. The inaccuracy of the name would be evident to people from Newcastle. Throughout the development of *Grounded* Alana took great care to ensure that the elements of the play that related to the city or to the events surrounding the grounding of the *Pasha Bulker* were always factually accurate. This was integral to ensuring the work maintained an authentic sense of place.

Apart from the title, and a slight change in character name, you'll see that the heart of the story remained steady throughout the two years of development. The initial proposal described the story in the following paragraph:

> *Tanker Town* is about a young woman, Aurora, who lives close to the Newcastle port. She is unpopular at school so she spends a lot of time watching the containers come in and out of the port, dreaming about other places where she might be able to get away to. Then one day, one of the container ships goes aground on one of the Newcastle beaches, and because of how much she knows about the ships and shipping she becomes a popular interviewee with the media. Indeed, the grounding of the ship brings the world that she has dreamed about for so long to her doorstep and Aurora realises that, however bad things get, it's never long before everything changes.

The proposal, and in turn the final script, caught our imagination because it used a unique and very specific Newcastle incident as the catalyst for a broader 'coming of age' tale. The notion of a teenage girl obsessed with the prospect of shipping is at the same time absurd and intriguing. It's plausible that someone growing up in one of the world's largest coal ports could become fascinated with the daily movement of ships from around the world. And it's equally plausible that such a person would be considered a 'freak' and an outsider by their peers. While we might not specifically relate to the interest ourselves, most people can relate to the sensation of being an outsider or looking for acceptance. As a result Alana had proposed an idea that could be at the same time specific to Newcastle but universally engaging.

As the development of the script got underway it became clear there were a number of obstacles to overcome. *Grounded* needed to weave together the actual events surrounding the grounding of the *Pasha Bulker*; find a way of communicating the importance of those events at the time; and then place this context within the fictitious journey of a teenage girl looking for a sense of acceptance or belonging. As the script developed Alana found a startlingly original way to counter these obstacles.

Alana Valentine is the only playwright I have worked with who sets the creative team presenting her work artistic challenges that she has not already resolved. So often one of the difficult things for a playwright seems to be that they have a very distinct idea of how their work should be presented. The tone of each sentence, the intentions and movements of the actors, even the layout of the stage can be vividly clear in the author's mind. When they attend rehearsals or performances there is a need to reconcile the difference between what they intended when they wrote a scene and the way the artists have interpreted their words.

Alana, by contrast, deliberately challenges artists presenting her work to find solutions to theatrical problems that she creates. I distinctly remember a conversation between Alana and the director of the play Toni Main. The stage direction states 'An ENORMOUS physical model of the *Pasha Bulker* crashes onto the stage' and Toni asked Alana how she imagined that happening. Alana's reply was simply, 'I don't know. You're the director, that's your job.'

Throughout *Grounded* Alana has used very different theatrical forms and conventions to convey the different aspects of the story. Farrah's closest relationships, those with Chloe and Jack, are represented in a naturalistic style that allows the audience to empathise and relate to her on a personal level. The style provides the emotional arc of the story as Farrah travels from isolation to a sense of belonging. All other relationships are represented in various forms to accentuate Farrah's difference or the emotional tone of the scene.

One of the interesting aspects of this play is the way the chorus is integrated into the action. The bullying that takes place at school is created by contrasting Farrah's naturalistic world with a stylised chorus who speak with different voices but a unified intention, clearly ostracising her from her peers. Similarly the direct impact of bullying on young people is represented by the chorus, but this time through the delivery of verbatim text recorded by Alana during script development workshops. The text provides very specific teenage voices talking about people who were picked on or isolated for being different. This text suddenly contrasts the often magical world of the play with the real life experiences of teenagers.

A scene that I find a particular theatrical delight is the grounding of the *Pasha Bulker*, which borrows very heavily from a traditional Greek chorus. During this scene the chorus transform into a highly abstract entity using language, rhythm and movement to convey the chaos and momentum of the storm. And then of course there is the second use of verbatim text to accurately convey the circumstances surrounding the event itself and the actions of the real-life people involved.

The character of Matilda, Farrah's mother, is represented by three actors in a single costume. Each of the actors represents one attribute of her mother's personality. Together they highlight the gulf that has opened between the two. Far from relating to each other as people, it becomes clear Farrah sees her mother as a creature very far removed from her own life. This theatrical device beautifully captures the sense that mother and daughter now live in different worlds.

Grounded breaks many theatrical conventions. There are two distinct stories interwoven: the journey of Farrah trying to reconcile her passion for shipping with the need to be accepted and loved by her peers, and the fascinating events surrounding one of Australia's most famous maritime incidents. These stories are fused together through a dynamic juxtaposition of theatrical styles.

For directors and actors this means there are nearly unlimited choices to bring this story to life on the stage. Alana has provided a rich theatrical blueprint to work from. But the ultimate success of the play relies on the amalgamation of her words and the participating artist's imaginations. You can't make obvious choices in staging this play because it wasn't written with obvious solutions in mind. You need to work it out. That is why this play is so exciting for directors, and why it is the perfect play to stage with young performers.

Fraser Corfield

Fraser Corfield is Artistic Director at Australian Theatre for Young People, Millers Point, Sydney.

Grounded was first produced by Tantrum Theatre at The Playhouse Theatre, Newcastle, on 10 May 2011, with the following cast:

FARRAH MARTIN	Jemima Webber
JACK	Mathew Baird-Steel
CHLOE	Siobhan Caulfield
MATILDA 1, 2 & 3	Tamara Gazzard, Emily Daly, Naomi Dingle
HARBOURMASTER / NIGEL	Paul Kelman
JIM	Scott Gelzinnis
JAMES	Dean Blackford
FIGURES 1–6	Emily Daly, Naomi Dingle, India Wilson, Tamara Gazzard, Dean Blackford, Scott Gelzinnis

Director, Toni Main
Designer, Marion Giles
Lighting Designer, Lyndon Buckley
Sound Designer, Allon Silove
Dramaturg, Fraiser Caulfield
Assistant Director, Rachel Jackett
Assistant Designer, Fern York

CHARACTERS

FARRAH MARTIN, 15
CHLOE, 15
JACK, 16
MATILDA 1, 2 & 3, Farrah's mother
HARBOURMASTER, Newcastle harbour
NIGEL, school librarian
JIM, 15
JAMES, 15
FIGURES 1–6

The the roles of Harbourmaster and Nigel are played by the same actor.

THANKS

The author would like to thank the many Novocastrians who contributed to the research and writing of this play, including Captain Timothy Turner, Newcastle Harbourmaster; Captain Timothy Delves; Captain Scott Curline; Captain Sandra Risk; Captain Andrew Beasley; Captain Phillip Hawke; Captain Lyndon Clark; Keith Powell; staff at Newcastle Public Library; and the Tantrum Ensemble participants from both of the workshops which took place in Newcastle in 2010/2011.

PROLOGUE

On a dark stage there are a dozen or more one-metre models of Panamax class bulk carriers, lit from within. As if we are looking at the Newcastle horizon at night, twinkling with the lights from all the vessels waiting to come into port.

FARRAH: It's a great place to grow up.
FIGURE 1: It's a boring place to grow up.
FARRAH: I really like it here.
FIGURE 2: I would so love to live somewhere else.
FARRAH: But I would like to get away.
FIGURE 3: Travel the world.
FARRAH: And then come back.
FIGURE 4: The centre of town is dying.
FIGURE 5: The burbs are the place to be.
FIGURE 6: The new hub.
FIGURE 1: Like the centre is probably going to come back.
FIGURE 2: That's going to take a very long time, and I'm gonna be out of here by then.
FIGURE 3: It's not totally bad or totally good. It just is.
FIGURE 4: Like there's a limit in Newcastle and by our age, you've already reached that limit.
FIGURE 5: So I plan to go.
FIGURE 6: Go.
FARRAH: Go.
FIGURE 1: I'm going.
FIGURE 2: Go. For sure.
FIGURE 3: I'm not saying Newcastle is terrible but I just don't think that I'd live here forever. I want to like leave and then come back when I'm heaps older.
FARRAH: Yeah, but that's what you don't understand.
FIGURE 4: I've got big plans. Big plans and as soon as I turn 18 I'm out of here. What are my plans? I dunno. But they're definitely big.
FARRAH: And that's all mine are too.
FIGURE 5: Newcastle is confused. It's a bit in love with the past and it's keen on the future but it's not sure how to get there.

FARRAH: If I had to say something?
FIGURE 3: If I had to tell someone something.
FIGURE 4: If I had to talk about living here.
FIGURE 5: I'd mention the beach.
FIGURE 6: I'd talk about the ocean baths.
FARRAH: I'd talk about the port.
ALL: The what?
FIGURE 1: You mean the tankers that go past Nobbys?
FARRAH: They're not tankers.
FIGURE 2: What's your problem?
FARRAH: I mostly keep it hidden.
FIGURE 3: Not really.
FIGURE 4: She's different.
FIGURE 5: She's just different.
FIGURE 6: Like a bit of an interest would be okay.
FIGURE 1: She just takes it too far.
FIGURE 2: For attention.
FIGURE 3: Because that's become her thing, you know.
FIGURE 4: Being different.
FIGURE 5: Kindy iffy.
FIGURE 6: Wired to the moon.
FARRAH: But you don't understand.
FIGURE 1: A few coconut crumbs short of the full lamington.
FARRAH: I'm the same as you.
FIGURE 2: And not good different.
FARRAH: Deep down I'm the same.
FIGURE 3: Odd different.
FIGURE 4: You know.
ALL: Farrah Martin she's a freak
    Stares at tankers every week
FIGURE 5: Spends her afternoons alone
FIGURE 6: Lives in a world all her own
FIGURE 4: We've tried to be nice to the little geek
FIGURE 5: But Farrah Martin's too oblique
FIGURE 6: We've tried to make her part of the groove.
ALL: Who knows what she's trying to prove?

> *A small group of* FIGURES *walk past the seated* FARRAH *and make the noise of a 'tooting' boat horn.* CHLOE *hurries over to* FARRAH.

SCENE ONE

CHLOE: Ignore them.
FARRAH: They were pretty loud.
CHLOE: We can still fix it.
FARRAH: I don't think so.
CHLOE: What you have to do is like not mention it at all for… just a while.
FARRAH: Okay.
CHLOE: Do you think you can do that?
FARRAH: Sure. I don't have to talk about it all the time.
CHLOE: Right.
FARRAH: I'm interested in other things.
CHLOE: Great.
FARRAH: I like the movies.
CHLOE: Apart from *Titanic*.
FARRAH: Yeah.
CHLOE: What?
FARRAH: *The Poseidon Adventure*. *The Hunt for Red October*.
CHLOE: They're like… both about ships.
FARRAH: One's about a submarine.
CHLOE: Yeah. Really different.
FARRAH: They are really different.
CHLOE: Nothing that has anything to do with water.
FARRAH: Right. Um. *Transformers*.
CHLOE: Great.
FARRAH: I'm really into *Transformers*.
CHLOE: Not too into it. You don't want them to think you've just transferred one obsession to another.
FARRAH: I dunno, Chlo.
CHLOE: You want to get invited to Tom's party, don't you?
FARRAH: Yeah.
CHLOE: So you're coming to the mall then?
FARRAH: For what?
CHLOE: For something to wear to Tom's party.
FARRAH: They're bringing the *Saga Ruby* in this arvo.
CHLOE: The what?

FARRAH: The *Saga Ruby*. It's a cruise ship built in 1973 in the UK, the last cruise ship ever to be built in the United Kingdom and this ship is just, I'm not kidding, it is just an absolute stunner. Like cruise ships usually look all boxy and square and this one is just pure elegance, the lines just sway around the vessel. The funnel is placed amidship and there's a sheer on the hull that is just, well it's just gorgeous.

CHLOE: No. No. NO!

FARRAH: What?

CHLOE: You can never talk like that. Ever.

FARRAH: But. How can I stop it? It just comes out.

CHLOE: Okay. When you feel yourself like about to say something about a ship just transfer it to a dress. Or a pair of shoes. So try it.

FARRAH: What?

CHLOE: The Saga Rubies are these shoes you really want.

FARRAH: And like platforms are just usually all boxy and square but these shoes are just pure elegance, with straps that just sway around the heels. The buckle is placed amid… strap and there's a shine to the leather that is just well, it's just gorgeous.

CHLOE: Not bad. Lose the 'amidstrap'.

FARRAH: Too much of a hint?

CHLOE: Way too much.

   Pause.

FARRAH: Seriously, Chlo, I don't know if I can do it.

CHLOE: You want to be like Natasha Green, who had to leave the school?

FARRAH: Of course not.

CHLOE: Then you've got to hide it. A bit.

FARRAH: You don't.

CHLOE: I do. Like 'cause I don't mind being a little bit unpopular, but I don't want to be totally dropped. You know.

FARRAH: I don't want to be totally dropped.

CHLOE: Then…

FARRAH: There's a shine to leather that is absolutely gorgeous.

CHLOE: Right.

FARRAH: And I'll go and get them tomorrow.

CHLOE: Farrah, you're not going out to the port.

FARRAH: Last time, I promise.

SCENE TWO

FARRAH *is leaning on her bicycle, referencing a book, when* JACK *rides in on a skateboard. For a moment he stands at the other side of the stage.*

JACK: Oi.

> FARRAH *ignores him.*

Hey, girl.
FARRAH: What?
JACK: What are you doing?
FARRAH: What's it to you?
JACK: You shouldn't be here.
FARRAH: Says who?
JACK: This is our place. Scoot your boot.
FARRAH: Does it have your name on it?
JACK: Yeah.
FARRAH: What are you, twelve?

> FARRAH *goes on reading.*

JACK: What's your book about?
FARRAH: Nothing you'd be interested in.

> *He comes closer.*

JACK: Looks like it's about boats.

> *She closes it quickly.*

FARRAH: No it's not.
JACK: I know you. You're that boat girl from school.

> *He snatches the book from her.*

FARRAH: Give it back.
JACK: Will you get in trouble if it gets damaged?
FARRAH: Give it back.
JACK: I will just tell me if you'll get in trouble.

> JAMES *and* JIM *enter on their bikes.*

JAMES: Who you talking to?
JACK: That boat-brain girl from school.
FARRAH: My name is Farrah.
JAMES: What are you doin' out here?

FARRAH: Nothing. I was just clearing my head. Going for a walk.

JACK throws the book to JIM.

JACK: Nothing with a library book.

FARRAH: Yeah.

JACK: Yeah. Ya like boats, do ya?

FARRAH: Not particularly.

JACK: I do.

FARRAH: Really?

JACK: Sometimes I just stand here and watch the tugs take those whopper tankers out through the mouth of the harbour past Nobbys.

He takes her by the cords of her hoody and pulls her forward.

I like it when the biggest tug leads the tanker right up to where the buoys are and then turns around and then it like goes backwards, so cool and then the tugs on either side keep going.

JIM comes over and gets on one side of FARRAH. JAMES comes over.

FARRAH: Then how about when they just slide it out the mouth of the harbour. Guide it through and then away it goes.

JACK: Gotcha.

FARRAH: What?

JACK: Knew I could get you to show us what a freak you are. All you have to do is mention tankers and she gets [*mockingly*] all choked up.

FARRAH: You know that they're not called tankers, they're called bulk carriers.

JIM: Oh, and I thought that was just your mother.

JAMES: Yeah, she's a bit of a bulk carrier, isn't she?

JACK: Why are you suddenly pretending that you're not into boats?

FARRAH: 'Cause I'm not.

JACK: Yeah, ya are. We know a boat-brain freak when we see one.

The boys circle FARRAH on their bikes and then they ride off.

SCENE THREE

FARRAH arrives at the library, slightly breathless. The librarian, NIGEL, is there to meet her.

FARRAH: I need a request for library purchase form.

NIGEL: No.

FARRAH: What do you mean, no?

NIGEL: We've run out.

FARRAH: Then I can do it online.

NIGEL: No.

FARRAH: No?

NIGEL: No, we can't order any more books about the history of, the construction of, the decommissioning of, the practices for the loading and unloading of, the tonnage of, the passage of, disasters of, or design of bulk carriers.

FARRAH: Why not?

NIGEL: People make other requests.

FARRAH: So?

NIGEL: People have interests other than shipping.

FARRAH: What?

NIGEL: Lots of things. Birds, plants, insects, costume design, woodwork, geography, travel.

FARRAH: So you can buy them as well.

NIGEL: People have begun to ask why all our new acquisitions are about shipping.

FARRAH: You may have noticed that we live in a port.

NIGEL: Yes and people want to read stories about crime and ancient Egypt and interior design in London.

FARRAH: Why?

NIGEL: Because they're not you, Farrah. Because they have an interest in things other than bulk carriers.

FARRAH: Why?

NIGEL: Okay, now I know you're being obtuse.

FARRAH: What's obtuse?

NIGEL: Well, if you would like to look it up in a dictionary I'd be only too happy to direct you to the reference section where you can see and open books about, miracle of miracle, things other than shipping.

FARRAH: Actually, I didn't want to order a book about ships.

Pause.

NIGEL: What are you doing?

FARRAH: What?

NIGEL: This is a trick.

FARRAH: It's not a trick.

NIGEL: You want to order a book about something other than shipping?

FARRAH: I do.

NIGEL: Nah, this is a trick.

FARRAH: It's not. [*Pause.*] Aren't you going to ask me what I want to order?

NIGEL: No. Because it will be a book that sounds like it's about something else but it's really about shipping.

FARRAH: Mr Cornwell?

NIGEL: Yes, Farrah.

FARRAH: Do you have holidays coming up?

NIGEL: What, like a working holiday as a seafarer on an Asia-bound container vessel?

FARRAH: Do you?

NIGEL: No. But I know that's the only kind of holiday you would be interested in hearing about.

FARRAH: Actually, I wondered if you had any books on leadership.

Pause.

NIGEL: Are you wanting to try for school captain?

FARRAH: No.

NIGEL: House captain?

FARRAH: No.

NIGEL: You sure?

FARRAH: I'm just interested in what makes people, you know, popular.

NIGEL: Popular enough to become school captain?

FARRAH: Whatever.

NIGEL: Well… there are books on management and there are books on group dynamics. But really if you want to learn about becoming a captain the best way to learn is from watching someone who is a leader.

FARRAH: Like who?

NIGEL: Well, I dunno. Is there anyone you know who is a leader?

FARRAH: No.

NIGEL: Someone in your class?

FARRAH: Not really.

NIGEL: Well, the books on management are in the centre aisle.
FARRAH: Thanks.

    NIGEL *exits*.

SCENE FOUR

CHLOE *enters and takes up a martial arts pose.*

FARRAH: What's happening?
CHLOE: The PE teacher is sick so kids from Year 11 are taking the class.
FARRAH: In what?
CHLOE: How do I know?
FARRAH: But who said they could?
JACK: What are we going to do?
JIM: SPEC
ALL: Spec
JAMES: SHOUT
ALL: Shout
JACK: SPEED
ALL: Speed
JIM: SOCK
ALL: Sock
JAMES: and SPILL.
JACK: What are we going to do?
ALL: Spec, shout, speed, sock and spill.
JACK: Not like that, you pussy.
JIM: Put some grunt into it.
JAMES: Are you here to learn self-defence?
JIM: or namby
JAMES: pamby
JIM: napkin embroidery?
ALL: Self-defence.
JACK: Then what are we going to do?
ALL: Spec, shout, speed, sock and spill.
JACK: Spec, shout, speed, sock and spill. Yes we are.
ALL: Yes we are.
JACK: Spec shout speed sock and spill. Spec. We are going to speculate

about places where and when we might need to use self-defence. Speculate. Activate those brain cells. Where might this happen. And speculate, what might I do. We're going to confront right now the possibility of reaching down and squeezing someone's balls.

JACK reaches out and squeezes one of the other figure's crotch.

Speculate. We're going to think about how it might feel to poke someone's eye…

He mimes doing so.

… bite someone's ear…

He mimes doing so.

… and bloody someone's nose.

He has mimed punching and smacking FARRAH through all of this speech.

'Cause if ya haven't thought about it you're gonna be too squeamish to do it when the time comes. We are going to shout. [*Loudly*] Back off! Stop that! Get lost!
ALL: Back off. Stop that. Get lost.
JIM: And who's that gonna scare? Not even the nerd who nicked your Butter Menthol, Nancy. Back off, stop that! Get lost!
JAMES: Back off, stop that! Get lost!
ALL: Back off! Stop that! Get lost!
JACK: Better. We're going to speed away. Poke them in the eye.

He does so.

Bite them on the ear.

He does so.

Bloody someone's nose and then run. Here comes the money, dudes and dudettes. Here comes the biff, herein is the bump, hands up for the sock it to them.

He has punched and smacked FARRAH through all of this speech.

We're going to target weak and vulnerable areas of the body. So if I grab you by the arm…

He does so and FARRAH pulls back.

… you are not going to pull back. You are going to lean in, pull your arm tightly to your body and wrench yourself out of that hold.

He gives FARRAH *a kind of chinese burn on the arm and struggles out of the hold.*

If I come up to you from behind and your attacker has you in a choking hold and you find you can't breathe you are going to…

FARRAH *is struggling to get out of the choking hold.* FARRAH *reaches back and pinches* JACK*'s thigh.*

Hey. Hey.
FARRAH: What?
JACK: Be cool.
FARRAH: Not in a fight.
JACK: In a fight class.
FARRAH: I'd beat you every time.
JAMES: Oooh. He's scared.
FARRAH: Good.
JIM: What's your problem, girl?
FARRAH: How come you're taking the class?
JAMES: The PE teacher is sick.
FARRAH: So why aren't we just having study time or something.
JACK: Because I offered to teach self-defence.
FARRAH: What, and you're a big expert, are you?
JACK: I've been learning since I was eight.
FARRAH: Doesn't make you an expert. I got away from you.
JACK: I let you get out of it.
FARRAH: Chances.

JACK *continues to hold onto* FARRAH*'s arm long past a 'reasonable' duration. His friends notice.*

JAMES: Let's get back to it, man.
JIM: Yeah, blow it off, dude.
JACK: Yeah. Whatever. [*Pause.*] Alright. What are we going to do?
JIM: SPEC
ALL: Spec
JAMES: SHOUT
ALL: Shout

JACK: SPEED
ALL: Speed
JACK: SOCK
ALL: Sock.
JACK: And spill your guts to someone when it's all over.

SCENE FIVE

FARRAH *is waiting outside* JACK's *class. He sees her and tries to walk the other way. She goes over to him. Still he hesitates.*

JACK: What are you doing now?
FARRAH: Waiting for you.
JACK: You'll need to join the queue.
FARRAH: No, I don't think I will.

Pause. JAMES *and* JIM *enter and come over to them.*

Jack, Jim and James. What are ya, the triple jays?
JACK: The Blue Jays.
FARRAH: The Blue Jays. How lame.
JACK: Says the girl who spends her afternoons staring at boats.
FARRAH: What exactly about that is such a threat to you?
JACK: Who said it was a threat?
FARRAH: Then why even bother hassling me?
JACK: You were in our spot.
FARRAH: I've never seen you there. So, what, you saw me there and that's when you decided it was yours?
JACK: What were you doing out there? Edge of the port? Girl all on her own. They're not gonna believe you were just looking at the shipping.
FARRAH: Why do you care what I do?
JACK: Why do you have to be so spiky?
FARRAH: What's that supposed to mean?
JACK: You're quite good-looking, is all I meant. You could afford to work that a little more, instead of setting yourself apart.
FARRAH: What sort of game is this?
JACK: Well, obviously one that you don't play very often.
FARRAH: So what would I have to do to become one of the Blue Jays?

Pause.

JACK: Where you going now?
FARRAH: Why do you want to know?
JACK: Where are you going?
FARRAH: The lighthouse out at Nobbys.
JACK: We'll meet you there in an hour.

SCENE SIX

CHLOE: You did what?
FARRAH: I told him I was going out to the lighthouse.
CHLOE: Do you like him, is that it? 'Cause if you do, this is not the way to get him.
FARRAH: I do not like him.
CHLOE: Yeah well, that's sometimes a sure sign you like him.
FARRAH: Lots of people like him. Lots of people follow him.
CHLOE: And is that why you waited for him after school?
FARRAH: Maybe I can learn some stuff from him.
CHLOE: Like what?
FARRAH: People do what he says.
CHLOE: Yeah, 'cause he's a bully.
FARRAH: He has charisma.
CHLOE: I just think he has a big mouth.
FARRAH: No, he has authority. Confidence.
CHLOE: He's got an out-of-control ego more like.
FARRAH: You want to be round him.
CHLOE: *You* want to be round him.
FARRAH: Wanna come with me?
CHLOE: I'm not traipsing all the way out to Nobbys.
FARRAH: Then why are you my friend?
CHLOE: I'm not. You're my friend.
FARRAH: I'm not into the White Stripes.
CHLOE: You want to be.
FARRAH: No, Chloe, I really don't.
CHLOE: Well, at least you understand why I am.
FARRAH: Not really.
CHLOE: Yeah, 'cause you feel about boats how I feel about them.
FARRAH: You're obsessed.
CHLOE: And you're not.

FARRAH: I don't wear captain's outfits to school. I've been trying to keep it more quiet.

CHLOE: In geography you look at coal distribution in NSW. In maths you do calculations based on tonnage and capacity. In English you do creative writing about life on the bulk carriers. It's… weird… serious weird shit.

FARRAH: Well, I'm still going out there.

CHLOE: Then he's really going to think you like him.

FARRAH: I said I was going to the lighthouse. He was the one who invited himself. If I don't go he'll think I'm scared.

CHLOE: And if you do go he'll think you're interested.

FARRAH: I am interested. In how he… you know… operates. How come he's the leader of the Blue Jays.

CHLOE: You do like him.

FARRAH: Not like that.

CHLOE: Yeah, you do.

FARRAH: There's a magic in it.

CHLOE: In what?

FARRAH: In getting people to follow you. In getting people to trust you. Imagine how much of that you'd have to have to be the captain of a ship.

CHLOE: Some people think you've got Aspberger's, you know.

FARRAH: Well, I don't.

CHLOE: Well, it might be easier if you said you did.

FARRAH: Other people are allowed to have hobbies.

CHLOE: But why ships. Farrah?

FARRAH: Why the White Stripes?

CHLOE: Because they're cool. Because she says it's okay to be different.

FARRAH: Because they're what you would be like if you could get out of here?

CHLOE: Partly.

FARRAH: Every day the world is coming in through the mouth of that harbour. Korean captains, Phillipino crew, beautiful old Empire line cruise ships full of Indians, and Mexicans and Norwegians. The White Stripes are your lifeline to what's possible. And these ships are mine. One day I'm going to sail away on one as a crewman and come back as third mate, then second mate, then first mate, then captain. I'm gonna sail in through that harbour mouth and I'll have seen all the spices and senses and spectacles of the world. You want to dress up and be strange, Chloe. Well, I want to sail away and be free.

CHLOE: I get that.

FARRAH: Yeah, I know.

CHLOE: Besties?

FARRAH: Sure.

CHLOE: Gotta have someone to share it with, huh?

FARRAH: I'll meet you at the mall to get those shoes.

CHLOE: Brilliant.

> CHLOE *exits.* FARRAH *stands on stage silently, listening to the* FIGURES *speak.*

SCENE SEVEN

FIGURE 1: This girl didn't do anything in particular. Just no-one liked her. It was horrible. People just ignored her. She was shut out of everything and when she left the school no-one even noticed.

FIGURE 2: He was actually a bit special and all the guys would just make fun of him constantly. The people who didn't make fun would try to ignore it but also laugh at the same time. So it wasn't doing evil, it was watching evil and not doing anything about it. Some shit went down later, they filmed him fighting other kids and it went all over YouTube. He graduated but sort of… hard. The whole journey was hard for him. But I still say hi to him at the bus stop.

FIGURE 3: He was special too but he wasn't that different. It was just that this was a kind of crueler making fun where he didn't understand they were making fun. Which can be worse.

FIGURE 4: There was a girl in my year and she was sort of obsessed with something as well and she was really different. She'd do weird things, but she was like… when I talked to her she was a really interesting and nice person. She was obsessed with Amy Winehouse but really, really obsessed.

FIGURE 5: It wasn't just Amy Winehouse… it was like…

FIGURE 4: She was like…

FIGURE 5: She was creative… she'd like get these thin little satin ribbons…

FIGURE 4: She'd get little blue satin ribbons and plait them all through her hair and I dunno some people weren't very nice to her. And then one

day she had this full-on outburst… she went like crazy at teachers and people who had been mean to her because she had this really good friend and other people were like a bitch to her and made her one friend not like her and then she didn't have anyone. So she had this full-on outburst, like she went crazy and then she pretty much stopped going to school.
FIGURE 6: Everyone can remember someone like that. Like at our school there was a girl who used to talk in an elf voice.
FIGURE 2: A what?
FIGURE 6: [*in an elf voice*] A little elf voice like this. Like she was a little elf.
FIGURE 2: That sounds a bit cool actually.
FIGURE 6: Nah.
FIGURE 1: The girl who left my school had a massive obsession with horses. Horses were like over everything she drew, on her folders and that kinda stuff. Her Myspace page of course. Her best friend drifted away from her. They were friends for years and then it was like over. No-one would talk to her. They'd sit away from her in class.
FIGURE 4: People did in the beginning pick on her but then it was like…
FIGURE 5: Avoidance.
FIGURE 4: Yeah avoidance, like…
FIGURE 5: She would walk and you'd just sort of move out of her way and you would never… some people would smile and stuff… no-one would ever be really rude or anything she was just never included… like she was picked last in PE and that sort of thing.
FIGURE 4: Like obviously I would think that she would like wanted to have friends. Who doesn't want to have friends?

SCENE EIGHT

The Blue Jays are waiting.

JIM: She's not coming.
JAMES: She's getting us back.
JACK: She'll come.
JIM: Nah.
JAMES: She's not coming.
JACK: She can't help herself.

JAMES: And why is that?
JACK: What?
JAMES: Why is she such a boat tragic?
JACK: How should I know?
JIM: Father figure.
JAMES: What?
JIM: You know.
JACK: Nah.
JAMES: Why nah?
JACK: 'Cause if you don't have a father you just get on with it. You don't miss what you don't have.
JAMES: Yeah, that's right.
JIM: Well, maybe she does.
JAMES: Nah.
JIM: She's pretty obsessed.
JACK: She's trying to stay a kid.
JAMES: What?
JACK: Like you know how when you're a kid you can get all nutzo about something… it's the same.
JIM: What did you get nutzo about when you were a kid?
JAMES: I dunno. He's telling the story.
JIM: Jack?
JACK: Dunno. I was into model airplanes for a while.
JIM: Yeah, I even liked stamps.
JAMES: Yeah, but you don't go all lame about them and bring them to school and bore everyone with talking endlessly about them.
JACK: Course I don't.
JAMES: Why not?
JIM: 'Cause I'm not some pea-brained, boat-brain nutzo, that's why.

Pause.

JAMES: So how does it hang onto her childhood?
JACK: I don't know. I'm just saying you do that shit when you're a kid and then you get over it.
JIM: When you want to grow up.
JACK: Maybe.
JIM: Yeah.

JAMES: So basically we're hassling her out of being a kid.
JACK: Right.
JIM: So we're doing her a favour really.
JACK: Yeah.

> *Pause.*

JIM: You never said.
JAMES: What?
JIM: What you were into.
JAMES: I wasn't.
JIM: Nah, it's because you still are.
JAMES: Am not.

> *They scuffle.*

JACK: Shut up. She's coming.

> FARRAH *comes on with a torch. The torch reveals graffiti on the side of the cliff before the lighthouse.*
>
> FARRAH *picks up a discarded spray paint can.*

FARRAH: Unbelievable.

> *There is a noise behind her and she turns.*
>
> JACK *is there taking a photo of her with his mobile phone.*

What are you doing?
JACK: [*in a high voice*] And what hour do you call this to turn up, madam?
FARRAH: What have you done?
JAMES: It's what we call outdoor canvas.
FARRAH: But why graffiti my name?

> *She throws the spray can at* JAMES. *Everyone freezes.*

JACK: I don't think she likes it.
FARRAH: I hate it. You've ruined it.
JAMES: That's not very nice.
FARRAH: Get it off, quick, before anyone sees it.
JIM: I'm a bit offended by that. I think you should apologise.
FARRAH: I'm not the one who needs to apologise.
JACK: We think it's really good.
FARRAH: You've got to get it off.

Pause.

JACK: Stay quiet and that'll be the end of it.

FARRAH: And I'm supposed to trust that, am I?

JACK: Trust shit. I said stay quiet and you can go about your tanker business.

FARRAH: They're not tankers.

JACK: What?

FARRAH: They're not tankers. They're bulk carriers.

JACK: Everyone calls them tankers.

FARRAH: Yeah, but that's wrong.

JACK: It's not wrong. It's just the common name for them.

FARRAH: No, actually it's wrong. Secondly, the tugs don't guide the tankers.

JACK: Of course they do.

FARRAH: No, the ship is being piloted and navigated under it's own steam. The tugs are there as risk management.

Pause.

JACK: Why'd you do that?

FARRAH: Do what?

JACK: Why'd you have to say that? Show me up for shit like that?

FARRAH: What did I do? Tankers are full of oil. This is a coal port. We have bulk carriers and container vessels. Not tankers. And the tugs do their main work at berthing, not during passage into the port.

JACK: We were being nice. Why can't you just be nice?

FARRAH: What do you mean, nice?

JACK: Play nicely. Don't… show people up for shit.

FARRAH: And what about you? You're supposed to be a leader. You're supposed to be… someone to look up to.

JACK: Since when?

FARRAH: I thought you were the boss of this crew?

JACK: Yeah? So?

FARRAH: So why are you pissing that away on bullying someone like me?

JACK: 'Cause that's the way it goes.

FARRAH: Not everyone can lead. And if you can… you should own it.

JACK: Says who?

FARRAH: You're not a leader. You're just a jumped-up thug.

JACK: Sticks and stones, little girl.

FARRAH: You want to know why I'm such a boat-brain, Jack? 'Cause captains are real leaders, real legends, real rock stars of the sea.
JACK: Crap they are.

Pause.

FARRAH: Listen, buddy, I was doing you a favour. You don't want to call them tankers to anyone who knows.
JACK: Yeah, good favour, freak.

The boys get on their skateboards and roll off.

FARRAH: It was a good favour.
JACK: Boat-brain.
FARRAH: Scum wad.

SCENE NINE

Three girls enter, identically dressed. They are Farrah's mother, MATILDA. *Each girl speaks separately; sometimes they speak together.*

MATILDA ALL: I don't need to listen.
FARRAH: But don't you want the truth, Mum?
MATILDA 1: Well, why would someone else spray your name?
FARRAH: I went there this morning and it had already been graffitied. I just picked up the can.
MATILDA 2: I don't believe you.
FARRAH: But don't you know that I would never graffiti something like that?
MATILDA 3: Then why did you have the photo on your phone?
FARRAH: One of them sent it to me, as a threat. You were never supposed to see it.
MATILDA ALL: Oh, I know that.
FARRAH: Why were you looking at my phone?
MATILDA 1: The school has told us to pay attention.
FARRAH: To snoop?
MATILDA 2: If we have to, yes.
FARRAH: So I just have no privacy?
MATILDA 3: If you haven't done anything wrong why do you need privacy?
FARRAH: Why are you being so ruthless with me about this?
MATILDA 1: I was shocked that you would do something like that.

MATILDA 2: You say you're looking at ships but you're actually a vandal.
MATILDA 3: And you must be hanging out with other vandals.
MATILDA 1: Because this is not like you.
MATILDA 2: Not the Farrah I know.
MATILDA Where did you even get the paint?
FARRAH: It wasn't me.
MATILDA 1: Then who was it?
FARRAH: It was this boy. These boys.
MATILDA 2: Your fellow vandals?
FARRAH: No.
MATILDA 3: Then how do you explain the photo on your phone?
FARRAH: You weren't supposed to see it.
MATILDA ALL: Oh, I know that.
FARRAH: It was their idea of a joke.
MATILDA ALL: I don't see that.
FARRAH: I know. It's not even funny.
MATILDA ALL: But this is what you do every afternoon while I'm at work.
FARRAH: No.
MATILDA 1: You're never here when I call.
FARRAH: Why do you call?
MATILDA 2: To check up on you.
FARRAH: Mum. You can't check up on me. You can't look in my phone.
MATILDA 3: I'm glad I did.
FARRAH: I just go out and look at the ships coming in.
MATILDA What?
FARRAH: I love going out there. I love it. I think a part of me would die if I couldn't go out there.
MATILDA ALL: God save us from teenagers and their weird obsessions.
FARRAH: It's not a weird obsession. It's a passion, alright. It's not a strange, dangerous perversion. It's an interest. I have an interest. Remember those? Back before you lost interest in everything and everyone.

Pause.

MATILDA 1: Well, I don't care what it is.
MATILDA 2: You're grounded.
FARRAH: This is so unfair.

MATILDA 3: No, Farrah, defacing a public place is unfair. If they trace it back to you do you know what kind of a fine I would face?
FARRAH: But I told you I didn't do it.
MATILDA 1: You were just looking at the ships.
MATILDA 2: Then why did you pick up the spray can?
FARRAH: If you'll just listen to me.
MATILDA ALL: I don't want to know.
FARRAH: Just listen to me!
MATILDA ALL: Don't you shout at me, Farrah.
FARRAH: Just listen to me. Please. [*Pause.*] It's these three boys, the Blue Jays.
MATILDA 1: They took the photo.
FARRAH: Yes.
MATILDA 2: Why?
FARRAH: Because… one of them is kind of interesting to me.

A long silence.

I thought I could maybe join up with them. I dunno.
MATILDA 2: And did you?
FARRAH: No.
MATILDA 3: No, instead I'm supposed to believe that you went out there and they set you up.
FARRAH: They're clever.
MATILDA 1: They're all clever. And when they're not clever, they're cruel.
FARRAH: You shouldn't have looked in my phone.
MATILDA 2: Who pays for it?
FARRAH: You do.
MATILDA 3: Well, while I pay for it I can look at what is being done with my money.
FARRAH: Fine.
MATILDA 1: You're not to go out there again?
MATILDA 2: To any part of the port.
FARRAH: Not at all?
MATILDA ALL: Not at all.
FARRAH: Please don't make me promise that.
MATILDA ALL: Promise me.

Pause.

MATILDA 3: You're thinking that you hate them. You hate that they have got you into trouble. My job here… my job as your mother is to tell you that it is not fair but that's the way it works. You can't go out there on your own otherwise they will hassle you. Yes. Stop it. They will hassle you and worse and people will say you were asking for it by being out there on your own. I know that's wrong. I know you've done it all your life. But that is how the world works. Do you understand me?

FARRAH: One last time.

MATILDA 1: Only to clean off the graffiti.

FARRAH: Fine. When?

MATILDA 2: I was going to say tomorrow morning. But I'd say you've got a pass because of the storm.

FARRAH: I don't mind a bit of wind.

MATILDA 1: Farrah, they've issued a severe weather warning.

FARRAH: Mum, if it's my last time. I'm going.

MATILDA 2: Let's see what the weather is doing in the morning.

FARRAH: I'm going.

> MATILDA *waits.*

Can I ask you one more thing?

MATILDA ALL: Go on.

FARRAH: Will you come out there with me sometime?

> *Pause.*

MATILDA ALL: Clean it off and come straight back.

SCENE TEN

The graffitied wall. FARRAH *begins cleaning.*

There is already a strong wind blowing and the signs of an approaching storm.

The FIGURES *enter. They are dancing and moving around like waves. Their hair is flowing like seaweed. They are seaweed creatures and barnacles and wind-whipped waves.*

FIGURE 6: Farrah Martin at the harbour's mouth
　The wind blows hard from the violent south
　The wind tears hard at the fringe of the land

The waves now smash on the fragile sand.
FIGURE 1: Farrah Martin, stubborn girl
Enough to make the seaweed curl.
FIGURE 2: Enough to make the fishes weep.
FIGURE 3: The waves are now a metre deep.
FIGURE 4: The waves are now a cliff of water.
FIGURE 5: She'll soon become old Neptune's daughter.
FIGURE 6: The force of the water roils and fights
And Farrah's face turns deathly white.
FARRAH: There. North-east, four nautical miles.
FIGURE 1: She sees the ship.
FARRAH: He's still got his anchor dropped.
FIGURE 2: She sees the ship in trouble.
FARRAH: He's still facing south. If he'd weighed anchor he would be facing east.
ALL: Who taught you that?
FARRAH: I taught myself.
ALL: The storm is coming. You should go in.
The storm is coming with raging wind.
FARRAH: But look, that bulk carrier is coming in even closer now.
FIGURE 1: He's trying to turn around.
FARRAH: No, he's not. What's he doing?

The storm begins around them in earnest and they huddle down.

There is wind and lights and water and noise—embellished with all the theatrical storm-making effects possible.

They are shouting above the sound of the howling storm.

ALL: You should go in.
FARRAH: Go in where?
ALL: Go into the lighthouse.
FARRAH: Are there…?
ALL: What?
FARRAH: Are there people?
ALL: Where?
FARRAH: In there?
ALL: In the lighthouse?
FARRAH: Right.

FIGURE 1: Electronic.
FARRAH: Detectors?
FIGURE 2: Electronic eyes.
FARRAH: Can I go in?
FIGURE 3: I don't know.
FARRAH: I can go in.
FIGURE 4: You won't damage anything?
FARRAH: No.
FIGURE 5: Can you see the…?
FARRAH: Yeah.
FIGURE 6: I think he's going to come in.
FARRAH: Do you think?
FIGURE 1: I hope not.
FARRAH: He'll turn it.
FIGURE 2: I hope so.
FARRAH: He'll turn it.
FIGURE 3: I don't think so.
FARRAH: That sea is so strong.
FIGURE 4: It is.
FARRAH: Look, it's coming in.
FIGURE 5: It's too strong.
FARRAH: I can't believe he would ground it.
FIGURE 6: But look at the swell.
FARRAH: I am.
FIGURE 1: He's coming in.
FARRAH: He's got to turn it.
FIGURE 2: Please turn it.
FARRAH: Turn it.
FIGURE 3: Look out.
FARRAH: It's the swell.
FIGURE 4: He's going to ground it.

> *An enormous physical model of the bulk carrier, the* Pasha Bulker, *crashes onto the stage. The size of the model should dwarf the characters so it might only be the bottom of the prow. But it should be astonishing and frightening for the audience.*

FARRAH: I think she's hit.
ALL: She has.

FARRAH: I think she's stuck.
ALL: She is.
FARRAH: She's stuck.
FIGURE 1: I can't believe it.
FARRAH: How bad.
FIGURE 2: I can't believe it.
FARRAH: How freakishly bad.
FIGURE 3: She's stuck.
FARRAH: She is.
FIGURE 4: She's stuck.
FARRAH: She is.
FIGURE 5: I never thought I'd see this in my lifetime.
FARRAH: I never thought I'd see this in my lifetime.
FIGURE 6: Let's go inside.
FARRAH: Would they know?
FIGURE 1: What?
FARRAH: The Port Authority, would they know?
FIGURE 2: Absolutely.
FARRAH: So they'll come.
FIGURE 3: They will.
FARRAH: They'll come and rescue the crew.
FIGURE 4: Yes.
FARRAH: How?
FIGURE 5: Helicopter.
FARRAH: In this weather?
FIGURE 6: They'll come.
FARRAH: I don't have to call?
FIGURE 1: No, they'll know.
FARRAH: Are you sure?
FIGURE 2: Yes, there are electronic eyes. They will have seen it go in.
FARRAH: Not like that.
FIGURE 3: Not like that.
FARRAH: That was terrible.
FIGURE 4: It was.
FARRAH: We should go inside.
FIGURE 5: Alright. Let's go in.

SCENE ELEVEN

FARRAH: I went into lighthouse and I was just gutted. Totally gutted. Because, well because it's the ultimate in any master mariner's career, isn't it? It's the absolute ultimate in failure to see his ship blown up on the beach. When I was standing there on Nobbys watching it all unfold, mostly I was just imaging how much that captain must have been panicking and the panic in that man's voice that the pilots must have heard on the VTIC must have been so pitiful. I was thinking 'why did you let yourself get in this position?' You know, 'you're a captain, you're supposed to look after your ship and your crew and you have a responsibility to keep your ship off our coastline, you know, because of what you can potentially do to it'. I was just overwhelmed by this feeling of being so let down by a captain, someone who I just automatically admire because they are a captain. You know, why are you letting this happen?

HARBOURMASTER: People who actually saw the ship come in said that she was literally driving toward the beach. They described how, when it was coming in the ship was in ballast, it hit the rock ledge like that bang and that instantly cut vast sections out of the ship's bottom, so a high percentage of the ship's ballast just dropped out, so the ship itself popped up, and that was the lurch people told us about. And then, exposed to the wind and the waves it got driven over the rocks, onto the sand and went bomp. If it hadn't hit the bit and cut the bit underneath, the water wouldn't have dropped and it wouldn't have popped up and it would have hit that rock and it would have just been totally destroyed. The ship would have fallen apart within an hour. So, as far as grounding a ship goes it was the most perfect grounding in history. The captain rode that ship in and all the gods were on his side. Having got to the point where he was definitely going to go onto the beach, it's a funny thing to say but the way it happened couldn't have happened better.

FIGURE 6: I got out of bed that morning and thought that the weather wasn't too hot. And although I wasn't on duty I had to go in and be on an interview panel for some positions with our VTIC which is the Vessel Traffic Information Centre. When I drive in I always drive along the beachfront and as you come along the beachfront to get into the pilot's station I just couldn't believe the state of the weather and what was more alarming was the fact that there were still ships closeish to shore in the anchorage. We always get these bad weather events that time of year and it's always common for a few ships to take their time to get out of the anchorage. And it's absolute madness because it's so dangerous to stay where they are. There's a fear of not going too far out, of the pilot boarding ground because I might miss my cue coming in and then my owner's going to be dark with me for the time delay. There's all these pressures that are applied to captains these days that are not just about the shipping conditions but are applied to them by masters sitting in head offices somewhere else.

FIGURE 2: I was in the pilot station to do these interviews with senior management and we ended up cancelling up because of the unfolding saga. We couldn't see anything from the Nobbys' camera because the wind and the rain was belting it around and on top of that we had limited tracking capabilities for the ships because radar gets knocked out with rain clutter. So at one stage I was tracking about six or eight ships that were dangerously close to shore and to be honest when the *Pasha* actually went on the beach I was relieved. Because I thought it should be alright and the crew would now be safe. The nailbiter was the *Sea Confidence* which almost went up onto the beach at Stockton. That went on all day and didn't end until 11 o'clock that night and it was just so close.

FIGURE 3: There was also another ship near Swansea that almost went up on the southern end of Redhead and Blacksmiths Beach. He was another one who couldn't get his anchor up, he was dragging toward the beach and he was starting to get quite panicky. We actually sent a tug out, the *Wickham* went out in absolutely foul conditions and headed down the coast to him. The guy up here near Stockton, he could see himself getting into trouble but he did some good things, he pumped emergency ballast to get the ship heavier in the water, when he realised he was probably going to go aground he put both his anchors out which is a dire straits thing to do and he hung on for grim death, I've got the photos of him bouncing around about a mile from Stockton Beach and people on the beach are just looking at this thing going 'shit, when is this thing going to come up on the beach?' So yeah, the *Pasha* was a secondary thing parked on the beach.

FIGURE 4: The whole focus became on how to refloat the *Pasha Bulker*. The salvage crew are not employed by the port, they're a whole separate crew. Trying to control the crowd was a huge job for the police and council. There was a shelter up at Nobbys and I saw a guy there for three days, he was taking photographs. He drove from South Australia just to get the best shot. And that wasn't unusual. I spoke to people from Brisbane, Tasmania, lots come up from Sydney. One day we had 250 journalists and photographers and we just didn't know how we were going to service all those people.

FIGURE 5: One day I had the producer from a breakfast program ring up and this is the first week and, um, wanted to make arrangements for her production crew to get on the bow of the *Pasha Bulker* because they were going to do the morning show from there. I thought this woman was joking until I realised she was serious. I said, 'do you realise what we're trying to do here?' They had no perception of the scale of the problem. She said to me 'imagine what we can do for you if you help me to do this', and I just said 'no thank you'. I said a number of times to the media 'this is not a media circus for you'.

FIGURE 6: A journalist rang up and said I'm gonna come up Thursday and I want you to spend two or three days with me so that I can write my story for this week's paper. I said, 'Mate, do you really realise what is happening here? You are one of two or three hundred journalists and you want me to spend two or three days with you.' He said 'Well, that's what my editor told me to do. He wants to do graphics of how the ship is going to be pulled off the beach.' 'Well, you can't do that because we don't even know so whatever you're going to do is going to be wrong. Don't do it.' I was pretty strong. In the paper there was the graphic of four tugs at the back pulling the ship off the beach. Completely wrong. Rang him for two days and never heard from him.

JACK: I was down there with the boys with the Jays, you know and there was all this media and they just wanted to talk to anyone, anyone who was local and I said 'yeah, I'm local', and then I dunno I threw in a couple of things about how they weren't tankers you know and how the tugs were there as risk management you know, and so they interviewed me about it and I was on the news. Yeah, on the evening news and yeah so then I started making stuff up, boat-brain shit you know about how my father used to tell me about the night when the *Sygna* came in on the beach and it was just some random shit I remembered from when we went to the museum with the school you know. But they wanted to talk to anyone. Anyone at all. It was fierce. We had a bit of fun with them. Boned up on shit we could get out of the library and we'd come up on the captions as local ship enthusiast. It was random but it was fierce. Nobody got hurt. Who cares, huh?

SCENE TWELVE

FARRAH *enters the library.*

NIGEL: Here you are.

FARRAH: What?

NIGEL: *Shipwrecks of the NSW Coast.* It's in.

FARRAH: Oh.

NIGEL: Oh. Is that all you can say?

FARRAH: Oh. Good?

NIGEL: I get asked for this book three times a day. Four times a day. I have to say 'No, it's on hold. One of our regular borrowers.' I've been holding it for a week.

FARRAH: Who asks for it?

NIGEL: Who doesn't ask for it?

FARRAH: *Shipwrecks of the NSW Coast*?

NIGEL: They're all out. Every book on shipping we have. Which, thanks to you, is quite a lot.

FARRAH: Right.

NIGEL: So.

FARRAH: So what?

NIGEL: So are you going to give me your library card?

FARRAH: Actually, I don't want to borrow it after all.

NIGEL: You don't want to borrow it?

FARRAH: No.

NIGEL: She doesn't want to borrow it.

FARRAH: No.

NIGEL: Let me guess. More management DVDs?

FARRAH: No, I'm good with that too.
NIGEL: What are you trying to do to me, Farrah?
FARRAH: How do you mean?
NIGEL: Are you trying to make me go completely insane?
FARRAH: No.
NIGEL: Then what's this about?
FARRAH: I dunno.
NIGEL: Just borrow it.
FARRAH: I won't read it.
NIGEL: Why?
FARRAH: I dunno.
NIGEL: So suddenly you've lost interest in all of this just as everyone else has finally noticed it's a port?
FARRAH: I dunno.
NIGEL: I thought this would be your finest hour.
FARRAH: Yeah. Me too.
NIGEL: But it hasn't?
FARRAH: No. It has.
NIGEL: What are you talking about? You were so obsessed. You were a freak.
FARRAH: Was I?
NIGEL: Maybe it was the being a freak you liked, more than the ships.
FARRAH: No, that's not it.
NIGEL: Sounds like it.
FARRAH: I didn't like being a freak.
NIGEL: Are you sure?

Pause.

FARRAH: No.
NIGEL: I'll put this out for general borrowing then.
FARRAH: Okay.

SCENE THIRTEEN

CHLOE: Why haven't you been at school?
FARRAH: I've been in bed.
CHLOE: Like flu or something?
FARRAH: Something.

CHLOE: You've got to come back to school.
FARRAH: Why?
CHLOE: You are like instant cool.
FARRAH: Am not.
CHLOE: Are so.
FARRAH: Why?
CHLOE: Because of this boat shit.
FARRAH: It's a ship.
CHLOE: It's a gift.
FARRAH: It's a disaster.
CHLOE: It's a boon. You're the bomb.
FARRAH: Really?
CHLOE: If you bothered to check your Myspace page you've got about 200 hits.
FARRAH: We don't have the internet on at home.
CHLOE: How poor are you, Farrah? Everyone has the internet on at home.
FARRAH: Fuck you.
CHLOE: Well, fuck you, get it on your phone.
FARRAH: With what?
CHLOE: I dunno, get a fucking shipping company to sponsor you, girl, you're a star. We're gonna get you talk to the media about all this boat shit. Okay, so when did you first see it?
FARRAH: I watched it happen.
CHLOE: On TV?
FARRAH: No, I was out there when it happened.
CHLOE: Out where?
FARRAH: At Nobbys lighthouse. I was cleaning off the graffiti and that's when I saw it.
CHLOE: You were out at the lighthouse.
FARRAH: Yeah?

   Pause.

CHLOE: Farrah, you don't need to make stuff up like that. You're already there.
FARRAH: I'm not making it up.
CHLOE: You were cleaning the graffiti and the storm came up and you just happened to be out there as the boat did its thing?

FARRAH: Turned full astern, backed up into the waves and was sent onto the reef.

CHLOE: You did not see that.

FARRAH: I did.

CHLOE: Oh, my God, you are going to be a rock star.

FARRAH: Why?

CHLOE: This thing has gone international, girl. There are people down there from interstate. Overseas. People are camping out to see it. They're going to so want to talk to you.

FARRAH: Have you seen it?

CHLOE: No. I'm not interested in that boat-brain shit.

Pause.

FARRAH: Neither am I.

CHLOE: We have to plan this. Like maybe you should call a media agent. I could call one for you. Like it sounds crazy but this whole thing is majorly crazy. What are you going to wear?

FARRAH: I'm not interested anymore.

CHLOE: Seriously, let me call 'Sunrise' or 'Current Affair'. I bet I can get you on them.

FARRAH: And say what? That someone I used to look up to just totally pissed on that?

CHLOE: What?

FARRAH: The ship is aground, Chloe. Even you must see that that's a total horror?

CHLOE: It's not that bad.

FARRAH: It is that bad. It's totally incompetent.

CHLOE: What do you mean used to look up to?

FARRAH: Nothing. Forget it.

CHLOE: I thought you looked up to the harbourmaster? What, you think he could have stopped it?

FARRAH: Not the harbourmaster, the captain of the *Pasha*.

CHLOE: You don't even know him.

FARRAH: He's a captain, Chloe. A captain. How could he do this?

CHLOE: I don't get it.

FARRAH: What if the White Stripes suddenly came out and said black, red and white were an evil colour combination or something.

CHLOE: Jack would never say that.
FARRAH: What if Meg did?
CHLOE: She never would. It's impossible.
FARRAH: Yeah, and if the impossible happened how would you feel?
CHLOE: But… you don't even know this guy.
FARRAH: Just shut up and piss off. I don't know why I'm friends with some White Stripes fan anyway. It's just retro punk shit. Get out of my face. Get out. Get out.

SCENE FOURTEEN

FARRAH *is sitting on her own.*

JACK: Hi.
FARRAH: Yes?
JACK: I just said hi.
FARRAH: What do you want?
JACK: Nothing.
FARRAH: Then get lost.
JACK: There's no need to be so aggro.
FARRAH: What? No posse with you today?
JACK: They're over at Nobbys.
FARRAH: With the rest of Newcastle.
JACK: So what are you doing out here?
FARRAH: I can be here. I can be anywhere I want. Dickhead.
JACK: Just turn it down, Farrah.
FARRAH: You hassled me.
JACK: I know. We were just being stupid.
FARRAH: You scared me. You shit.
JACK: So I'm sorry.
FARRAH: Too late.
JACK: Come on.
FARRAH: Don't tell me come on. Don't tell me that.
JACK: Alright.
FARRAH: You think you can just say 'sorry' and that's it. I'm not even supposed to be out here. I promised my mother I wouldn't come out here. And she only told me I couldn't come because of you.
JACK: Me?

FARRAH: Like you. People like you.

JACK: Alright.

FARRAH: I promised. I promised my mother. And I still came out here.

JACK: So, don't tell her.

FARRAH: Great. So I become a shitty little liar like you.

JACK: Farrah, listen, I've tried to say sorry, alright? We weren't going to hurt you. We were just trying to scare you a bit.

FARRAH: Why?

JACK: For a laugh.

FARRAH: And what's today about? You want to scare me again? You want to make my mother never trust me again?

JACK: Farrah, you sound a bit crazy.

FARRAH: Yeah, I am.

JACK: Quit it.

FARRAH: You scared now.

JACK: Quit it.

FARRAH: So what are you doing here?

Pause.

JACK: I wanted to see if you wanted to hang out. For real.

FARRAH: What?

JACK: Forget it. You're still too pissed off.

FARRAH: Hang out?

JACK: Yeah.

FARRAH: Like what?

JACK: Like nothing. Like hang out and talk.

FARRAH: Talk about what?

JACK: Nothing.

FARRAH: 'Cause I'm not into ships anymore.

JACK: How come?

FARRAH: Grown out of that shit.

JACK: No you haven't.

FARRAH: Maybe I have.

JACK: Nah.

FARRAH: How do you know?

JACK: Because I know how they make ya feel.

FARRAH: Oh, yeah.

JACK: Weak.

FARRAH: You'd like that.

JACK: They make ya feel weak and small.

FARRAH: And that'd be good, would it?

JACK: Yeah, because ships aren't just beautiful. They're sublime.

FARRAH: Listen to it.

JACK: Don't do that.

FARRAH: What?

JACK: Take the piss.

FARRAH: Well, come on. Sublime?

JACK: Yeah, and what word would you use?

FARRAH: Go on.

JACK: Sublime. Beyond something being beautiful is a feeling of smallness, of delight in being dwarfed. Like by a mountain.

FARRAH: Have you… I mean… have you felt that?

JACK: Yeah.

FARRAH: Yeah?

JACK: It's about like accepting that not everything that's more, you know, powerful than ya needs to be, I dunno… bad.

FARRAH: Yeah.

JACK: Like I don't like it when the Head makes ya feel small, or some witch in the servo or some pooncey mobile phone plan nob. But a ship like the *Pasha*, like the ones you dig, they're awesome.

FARRAH: Noble.

JACK: Sure.

FARRAH: Mmm.

JACK: Is that what got you into them?

FARRAH: I get the small thing, you know. Like and when I would look at the ships you know I'd feel small too but not small small like I'd handle it. Like when I was small next to a ship it was like cool to be small or something, you know.

JACK: Yeah, and I reckon that's what the *Pasha*'s made everyone in Newcastle feel, hey. It's such a huge cock-up and it makes cock-ups I've done, like hassling people and then feeling really lame about it, it makes them seem less lame… like. That's why everyone's been so happy..

FARRAH: I haven't.

JACK: Why?

FARRAH: Dunno.
JACK: Sulking.
FARRAH: I'm not.
JACK: But you've been into boats ever since your dad left. Sorry.
FARRAH: You don't even… He didn't even leave.
JACK: Yeah, he did.
FARRAH: You don't even know that.
JACK: That's what Chloe told me.
FARRAH: Chloe. What?
JACK: She told me that you miss your dad.
FARRAH: I don't even know him, okay.
JACK: What, never?
FARRAH: A while ago. But that doesn't count.
JACK: But you want to.
FARRAH: Well, I'm sure he's happy now with some… you know… on a ship somewhere… sailing away… with the salt in his hair… but in a good way.
JACK: And is that where you want to be?
FARRAH: Look, it's just an interest. I'm not obsessed and I'm not weird.
JACK: I like boats. Not like you. I like skateboards, but I'm not obsessed. My dad helped me build it.
FARRAH: Lucky you.
JACK: So… you want to go down and see the *Pasha Bulker*?
FARRAH: Why?
JACK: Just to hang out. Together.
FARRAH: Yeah. Okay.

SCENE FIFTEEN

The FIGURES *enter, they are a mosh pit crowd and* CHLOE *is a rock star, microphone in hand, rapping the poem.*

FIGURE 1: But just for love does Chloe send an email to the man.
CHLOE: My friend was out on Nobbys when the *Pasha* came to land.
My friend was in the wind and rain and saw the ship aground.
Then went inside the lighthouse to watch it toss and found.
My friend can give an eyewitness account of all she saw.
You're probably someone who won't find it all a bore.

My friend she's not so popular because she's into ships.
And all the peer rejection has turned her into quite a bitch.
Since the *Pasha* grounded she's been off without a trace.
The other day she yelled at me to get out of her face.
And now I don't have any friends to talk to through the week.
I think it would be really good if you agreed to meet.
I know you're really busy and don't have time for this
I know you're an important man with a super long 'to do' list
But she's my only friend you see and it wouldn't be a chore.
'Cause maybe it's of interest to know all the things she saw.
And maybe you can tell her that it was Chloe who wrote to you
And maybe that would make us find a way to start anew.

> CHLOE *turns and falls backward into the arms of the crowd who carry her off.*

SCENE SIXTEEN

FARRAH *and her mother,* MATILDA, *enter.*

MATILDA ALL: You're not ready.
FARRAH: I'm not going.
MATILDA ALL: Are you sure?
FARRAH: Yep.
MATILDA 1: You've wanted to meet the harbourmaster all your life.
FARRAH: She shouldn't have written to him.
MATILDA 2: Why not?
FARRAH: It's so embarrassing.
MATILDA 3: I think it was a very nice thing to do.
FARRAH: She did it to spite me.
MATILDA 1: I don't think so.
FARRAH: Yeah, she knew it would really embarrass me.
MATILDA 2: I think that's unkind. Very unkind.
FARRAH: Well, why would she think I'd even want to meet him?
MATILDA 3: Even I know you want to meet him.
FARRAH: He'll ask me.
MATILDA ALL: What?
FARRAH: Whether I want to be a marine pilot or not.
MATILDA ALL: Then tell him.

FARRAH: I don't know.
MATILDA ALL: You must have some idea.

Pause.

FARRAH: I can explain it but you won't understand.
MATILDA ALL: Try me.
FARRAH: It's like I'm stuck on dead slow ahead. The swell has risen and the pilot has called dead slow ahead and even with the engine running I'm not moving.
MATILDA 1: You're right. I've got no idea what you're talking about.
FARRAH: Imagine I'm a fish and I'm swimming upstream and the current coming the other way is so strong that I'm swimming as hard as I can but I'm not going anywhere.
MATILDA 2: Why not?
FARRAH: Because. Because I've always been so sure what I wanted to be.
MATILDA 3: Okay.
FARRAH: And now I'm unsure.
MATILDA 1: It's alright to be unsure.
FARRAH: It's not. Because I'm not just unsure about one thing. I'm unsure about everything. All at once.
MATILDA 2: Unfortunately, darling, that's what making a decision is all about.
FARRAH: But how can you make a decision that will affect everything about your life?
MATILDA 3: Stop trying to decide and just see.
FARRAH: Just wait for the tide?
MATILDA 1: If you like.
FARRAH: I'm the one who's grounded here, Mum. I'm high and dry. I'm not just going to float off with the tide. And I feel like I might break into a thousand pieces.
MATILDA 3: Honestly.
FARRAH: What?
MATILDA 1: You need to calm down, Farrah. You're not grounded. You're just negotiating your way down a very narrow channel.

FARRAH laughs.

MATILDA 2: What?
FARRAH: You're describing it in shipping terms.

MATILDA 3: Well, that's all you seem to understand.
FARRAH: Was he a seaman?
MATILDA 1: Who?
FARRAH: My father.
MATILDA 1: Yes. You know he was a sailor.
FARRAH: A steward or a deckhand?
MATILDA 1: Do you know I don't even know.

Pause.

FARRAH: Why haven't we ever talked about him?
MATILDA 1: 'Cause I guess I'm ashamed of how little there is to tell. You were the baby I wanted and I guess I always thought that would have to be enough.
FARRAH: I know you wanted me.
MATILDA 1: More than anything in the world.

They embrace.

Go on.
FARRAH: What?
MATILDA 2: Go and find out when they're going to get that boat off my bloody beach.
FARRAH: It's not a boat.
MATILDA 3: Yeah. I know.

SCENE SEVENTEEN

FARRAH *and* HARBOURMASTER.

HARBOURMASTER: Hi, I'm Franklin Fitter.
FARRAH: Hello. You're Captain Fitter.
HARBOURMASTER: Nice to meet you.
FARRAH: You're the harbourmaster.
HARBOURMASTER: That's right.
FARRAH: Really?
HARBOURMASTER: I understand that you want to be a marine pilot, Farrah.
FARRAH: It was a phase.
HARBOURMASTER: I beg your pardon?
FARRAH: It was a phase I was going through.

HARBOURMASTER: I understood it was more than that.

FARRAH: Turns out it wasn't.

HARBOURMASTER: Oh. Okay. [*Beat.*] So what are you going to do now?

FARRAH: I'm not sure. All I ever wanted to do was go to sea.

HARBOURMASTER: Better to find out before we invest all that money in you.

FARRAH: I guess.

HARBOURMASTER: Thousands of dollars to train every pilot who works in this port.

FARRAH: But considering the hundreds of millions of dollars in shipping they're handling that's not a lot.

HARBOURMASTER: That's right. And 23 is the number of pilots working too.

FARRAH: Twenty-four counting you. Because you're still active.

HARBOURMASTER: You're well informed.

FARRAH: For an amateur.

Pause.

HARBOURMASTER: I understand you were out on Nobbys the day the *Pasha* was grounded.

FARRAH: Yep.

HARBOURMASTER: That must have been a pretty exciting story to tell your friends. I'm surprised I haven't seen you in the media.

FARRAH: I didn't think it was right to speak about it.

HARBOURMASTER: Right?

FARRAH: No.

HARBOURMASTER: I don't understand.

FARRAH: I watched the humiliation that went on in the media, tearing the captain to shreds over it and I watched the joking that went on and all the rest of it and it made me really sad. Because, as a professional mariner that's such degrading thing to happen to someone. Because the public and the media are more than happy to tear someone to shreds when they've done the wrong thing but nobody talks about all the times when ships are brought in in bad weather completely safely. I actually felt disgusted to live in a culture where it's okay to rip people to shreds when there's been a disaster but the day-to-day job that pilots do just goes completely unnoticed. People only take an interest when something goes wrong. Yeah. So that's why I didn't want to say anything. [*Pause.*] What?

HARBOURMASTER: You're sure you don't want to work for me?
FARRAH: Nah.
HARBOURMASTER: Too scared?

> FARRAH *nods*.

'Cause look what can happen to you, huh?

> FARRAH *nods*.

And you're gonna add to that masters who'll refuse to be brought in by a female pilot, and when you're at sea, you're gonna add maybe being one of the only women on a ship and you're gonna add the possibility of pirates boarding and being one of the only women on a ship.

FARRAH: Yeah.
HARBOURMASTER: And you're gonna add fires at sea and when you're third mate having to possibly perform medical procedures on your male colleagues and possibly having to perform medical checks on rescued foreign male seafarers.
FARRAH: Oh.
HARBOURMASTER: And you're gonna add some moral questions because Newcastle is the biggest coal port in the world and you're gonna wonder about contributing to the world's pollution like that. I'm not saying you're gonna be a greenie, I'm just saying it's gonna occur to you that you are part of that chain.
FARRAH: Yeah.
HARBOURMASTER: So you've got a lot of things to consider.
FARRAH: Mmm.
HARBOURMASTER: Like what?
FARRAH: What?
HARBOURMASTER: If you had to bring the *Pasha* back into this port what would you consider?
FARRAH: First I'd consider the tidal range.
HARBOURMASTER: Why?
FARRAH: Because the bigger the tidal range the larger the current that's flowing. The current affects how the ship handles on the water and how much you're getting pushed around by the current.
HARBOURMASTER: And I bet you know what the tidal range is in Newcastle port, don't you?

FARRAH: The highest astronomical range here is 2 metres, 2.1 but that's a rare circumstance, you don't normally get much above 1.7, 1.8 metres.
HARBOURMASTER: What else?
FARRAH: Is the rudder working?
HARBOURMASTER: No.
FARRAH: I would assume it would have been sheared off when it hit the reef.
HARBOURMASTER: Actually when we were getting it off the reef.
FARRAH: Right.
HARBOURMASTER: You've got a basically dead ship with no propellor blades and no prop shaft. Anything else?

Pause.

FARRAH: I'd also consider the amount of freshwater in the harbour.
HARBOURMASTER: Very good. The freshwater sits on top of the saltwater, some of it mixes in but the bulk of it sits there like an extra buffer you've just got to push against.
FARRAH: Right.
HARBOURMASTER: But that was really sharp to think of that.
FARRAH: Thank you.
HARBOURMASTER: Really. You're good. You could do this.

FARRAH *bites her lip to stop herself from crying.*

FARRAH: Thank you.

SCENE EIGHTEEN

CHLOE *is seated when* FARRAH *holds a large peppermint swirl on a stick.*

CHLOE: What's that?
FARRAH: You tell me.
CHLOE: It's a peppermint swirl.
FARRAH: Which the White Stripes have been using for their 'Icky Thump' tour promotion.
CHLOE: They always use a peppermint swirl.
FARRAH: Yeah.
CHLOE: So what's so special about this one?
FARRAH: Have a look.

CHLOE *looks at it.*

CHLOE: 'Icky Thump' tour pins. Where'd you get these?
FARRAH: Ordered them online.
CHLOE: But you can't get them except on the tour.
FARRAH: Thought that might make you crack a smile.
CHLOE: Nah, that's the advantage of being a retro punk, you never have to crack a smile.
FARRAH: I shouldn't have said that.
CHLOE: Why not, it's what you really think.
FARRAH: It isn't.
CHLOE: Then why'd you say it?
FARRAH: Because I'm a total idiot.
CHLOE: And why are you here? Aren't they bringing in that stupid bloody ship today.
FARRAH: Yeah.

Pause.

CHLOE: There's no way.
FARRAH: Come on.
CHLOE: Forget it. I thought we could get back to… you know… how we were, but now I'm not so keen.
FARRAH: There's going to be half of Newcastle out there, all along the breakwater, right round past the Crown Plaza. It'll be something to see.
CHLOE: A big damaged ship. So what?
FARRAH: Chloe, how often have the White Stripes been to Newcastle?
CHLOE: Never.
FARRAH: And if they came do you think I'd come to see them with you?
CHLOE: I don't care.

Pause.

FARRAH: Get behind me, Satan.
CHLOE: Yeah, you should.
FARRAH: Yeah, I am.
CHLOE: And if anyone else would be friends with you, you wouldn't bother with me.
FARRAH: Who else would be friends with me?

CHLOE: No-one.
FARRAH: No-one in their right mind.
CHLOE: You saying I'm crazy now?
FARRAH: If the cap fits.
CHLOE: You're just as crazy.
FARRAH: That's right. And I've had no-one to share it with. No-one. You don't even know what I've been through these last few weeks. Because when that ship grounded it was so foul. And I just wanted it to go away. But it was like every day was another reminder of how dumb I'd been to think I could ever get away from here and meet someone, anyone who doesn't think that being into ships is just the stupidest thing for a girl to be into.
CHLOE: Well, at least you've been practising your violin.
FARRAH: What?
CHLOE: Feeling sorry for yourself and playing the smallest violin in the world.

She holds up her hand and plays the violin between her forefinger and thumb.

FARRAH *begins to leave.*

Wait. What about my peppermint swirl?
FARRAH: Here.

She hands it to her. CHLOE *looks at it.*

JACK *enters.*

JACK: Got one for me?
CHLOE: You a White Stripes fan?
JACK: Not really.
FARRAH: Hi, Jack.
JACK: Hi, Farrah. Whatcha' doin?
FARRAH: We were just heading down to see the *Pasha* come in.
CHLOE: You go with him. Don't worry about me.
FARRAH: Come on. We can both go with him.
CHLOE: Nah. I'm not really interested.

JACK *and* FARRAH *act out the following disaster scenarios.*

JACK: You know that when they pull it off the reef it might break apart.
CHLOE: Yeah?

JACK: Like right down the centre. Imagine that.
CHLOE: That would be pretty spectacular.
JACK: An' all the oil comes glugging out in one giant whoosh. Bam!
FARRAH: Won't be doing surfing at Nobbys next semester.
JACK: Word up.
FARRAH: And even if they get it off without that happening, there's no engine and no steering.
JACK: So instead of coming in all straight through the entrance it might go out of control and take out the breakwater.
FARRAH: Bam!
JACK: And if it's still wheeling around, out of control, it might take out the pilot station.
FARRAH: Smash!
JACK: And if they can't get the speed up and it's totalled all along the harbour, they might accidentally jam it through one of the barriers so that it ends up in the park.
FARRAH: Leaking oil all over the park.
JACK: Yeah, or it might sink, right there in the harbour entrance.
FARRAH: Fwooh!
JACK: Right there and it just sinks and no ships can get in or out for months.
FARRAH: Whoa!
JACK: And if the tugs lose control of it it might be this giant out-of-control ship, spinning wildly until it suddenly…
FARRAH: … with an eerie creaking sound…
JACK: … rrrhhhhhhhahhh…
FARRAH: … falls over on its side and crushes the thousands who have lined the foreshore to watch it come in.

They tip over and fall on top of CHLOE. *They all get up, laughing.*

CHLOE: You really think something might go wrong?
FARRAH: Sure.
JACK: Either way it's gonna be chronic.
FARRAH: A real woot fest.

CHLOE *looks at* JACK *and then* FARRAH.

CHLOE: Yeah, alright then.
JACK: Alright what?

CHLOE: Where do you want to watch it from?

SCENE NINETEEN

FIGURE 1: That morning, when I was about to bring the ship in, the swell was down and the wind was looking a bit dodgy and there was the forecast of a front to come through later in the morning.

FIGURE 3: The *Pasha* was way out in the Stockton bight with the salvage tugs and by this stage the wind was up to 35 knots from the west, the north-west, it was really starting to blow. And I was thinking we're probably going to have to delay the entry of the ship until the wind eases off.

FIGURE 4: I remember getting out of the helicopter and walking along the deck of the *Pasha* and the other pilot, Scott, said to me 'what do you think?' and I said 'ah well, it's a bit breezy, I suppose'.

FIGURE 5: Anyway we climbed our way up to the bridge and I went through the passage plan with the salvage master and the actual captain of the *Pasha Bulker*, the Korean captain, he was there but very much in the background. I outlined to the salvage master what I was going to do. And when I got my pen out my hands were shaking and I was surprised, I didn't think I'd be that nervous but I was.

FIGURE 6: The salvage master was concerned like I was about the wind conditions which at that stage were gusting up to about 46 knots and he'd just turned the ship around in a big turn to allow us to land on it in the helicopter and as a result he'd lost all speed, it was down to, when we started the piloting, it was down to a speed of about two and a half knots.

ADULT: I knew I wouldn't be able to get the ship in safely with that sort of speed so I guess that's when you call on your experience over many years of working this pond and all the ship-handling skills that you've got. So I called another one of the tugs out who wasn't supposed to be assisting with the *Pasha* and I hooked him up. When the speed got up to 4.6 knots I was a lot happier and we headed for the breakwater. And that was when I saw that more than half of Newcastle was out there there watching me. It was just mind- blowing and… it was a very public job. Three quarters of Newcastle were out there on the foreshore! They were all down

Stockton side, they were right from Nobbys breakwater, all the way down to Crown Plaza. So I get to the entrance of the harbour, the ship starts rolling off a bit to port, but we got through the entrance no problems at all and I thought this is pretty good. We were coming down past Nobbys toward the pilot station and I'm trying to co-ordinate six tugs.

CHLOE: Why is he going so fast?

FARRAH: If you keep the speed on you have more control.

ADULT: When it's slower the ship tends to skate and blow around. But if you have too much speed your tugs can't hold you in position. But I looked up at the foreshore and there were just people everywhere and I remember thinking 'If I stuff this up I'm gonna be on every television news program in the world tonight'.

FARRAH: If he stuffs this up he's going to be on every television news program in the world tonight.

ADULT: But no pressure, you know. Because I was thinking this is right up there. And I'd never done anything like it before. But I remember looking at all those people and thinking what a big deal it was for Newcastle so I said to the salvage master, 'have we got a whistle for the ship?' because normally we blow the whistle as we go around the corner and he said, 'no, we've got nothing working at all', so I called up all the tugs and I said, 'on the count of three all blow your whistles', and I went, 'one, two, three'.

The FIGURES *all make the sound of the tugs' whistles (or it could be a taped sound effect).*

And we did it again halfway again as we were going across the horseshoe.

The FIGURES *all make the sound of the tug whistles again.*

Because everyone was waving and everyone was just so elated to see the thing off the beach and finally in a safe position and just after we did the second one the harbourmaster rings me from the incident control room and says…

ALL: 'You gotta do it again.'

ADULT: Everyone was really going berserk so we did it again just as we were approaching the Crown Plaza.

The FIGURES *make the sound of the tug whistle and cheer.*

FARRAH: Then he took it round and put it up against the wharf and they had webcams set up throughout the harbour broadcasting this live on the web. So he tied it up against the wharf and threw an oil spill boom around it and everybody just went off and had a night of celebration. Because everyone had had enough of it by that stage.

NIGEL: Name for me if you will the marine pilot who safely brought in the *Pasha Bulker*?

FIGURE 5: It's not on the internet.

HARBOURMASTER: It wasn't in the papers.

FIGURE 4: There was no '60 Minutes' feature profile.

FIGURE 1: There was no mention in the Queen's Birthday honours.

HARBOURMASTER: A job that goes unnoticed and unmentioned.

NIGEL: A quiet, careful work of immaculate skill and utter precision.

HARBOURMASTER: A sliding through velvet dark water in the still of night.

FIGURE 4: While Newcastle sleeps.

FIGURE 2: While Newcastle works.

NIGEL: Ships do their delicate dance on sunlight-spangled waves.

HARBOURMASTER: Turning on the head of a pin.

FIGURE 4: Tug boats nudging them into berth.

FIGURE 3: Lines tied and rat guards mounted.

NIGEL: In wind-whipped weather.

HARBOURMASTER: The helicopters hover over rocking decks.

FIGURE 3: Pilots mount ladders and climb to the deck.

FIGURE 4: Pilots climb staircases up to the bridge.

FARRAH: And she asks herself
   am I one who watches
   who longs to sniff the salt air as my morning breath
   who sees the wind whip her bedroom curtains
   and longs to be out on the churning green sea
   am I one for whom the ships whistle blows
   a hard clear call
   who harkens to the cry of gulls
   and the wash of waves on a summer line load.
   Am I the one?

SCENE TWENTY

The FIGURES *become a 'group' of school friends, sitting in a circle, with* FARRAH *apart from them.*

FIGURE 1: I think I would like to go into advertising because I love design and I love writing and you have to do both of those things. And there's a really strategic side to it which is what I also love.

FIGURE 2: I thought I wanted to be a drama teacher but lots of things have happened and I've swapped around to public relations. Because that's only a two-year course and I don't want to have to do the four years that drama teachers have to do.

FIGURE 3: I dunno. I guess I'll try and get a job somewhere else. I don't even want to go to uni in Newcastle. I mean, for me, that's not what I want.

FIGURE 4: I get so sick of this question.

FIGURE 5: Like from the age of 12 you're asked 'so what are you going to do?'

FIGURE 4: Try from the age of five.

FIGURE 5: Yeah, I have no idea what I want to do and I'm gonna choose my courses for Year 11 based on what I like, but I don't know what I'm gonna do in Year 12. Or after. I'll probably do a Bachelor of Arts and take everything a year at a time and just kind of go with it and see.

FIGURE 6: Some people just know what they want to do.

FIGURE 1: Like Farrah.

FARRAH: Yeah.

FIGURE 6: Since we've got to the end of Year 10 I've started to see how cool that is.

FIGURE 5: Like Farrah has just always known and she's been really focussed while we were like…

FIGURE 4: … still being kids.

FIGURE 5: But she's never wavered.

FIGURE 6: That's so cool.

   FARRAH *goes over and sits with them.*

FIGURE 3: Like travelling is one thing that I really want to do. And I don't know if that's travel for work or just travel to see, you know.

FARRAH: I've always wanted to travel.

FIGURE 2: Aren't they building a VFT for Newcastle?
FIGURE 3: What's that?
FARRAH: A very fast train.
FIGURE 2: That will make a massive difference to where people will want to live. And like, 25 minutes to Sydney. Why would you want to live there when you can live here and be so much more relaxed?
FIGURE 4: Is it going to be 25 minutes?
FIGURE 1: That's so fast.
FARRAH: Actually, it's not really that fast compared to a lot of VFTs overseas but it is still fast for Newcastle.
FIGURE 3: I just don't want to be stuck here. Because there's so many other opportunities out there. I mean, I really like the place, I have a lot of friends and a lot of family here but it's just not enough.
FARRAH: It's like if you want to make something of yourself you've got to leave here before you can come back so you've got a worldly experience.
FIGURE 1: Because if you just stay in the one place you don't know anything.
FIGURE 2: Even though you might.
FIGURE 3: But that's what people make you feel as though… if you don't move out of home and go overseas, you know, you haven't lived.
FIGURE 4: That's my exact problem with what I want to do. Because obviously I'm a person who likes to be in control of things and take charge of things but I want someone to show me what is possible that I haven't even thought of.
FIGURE 5: Like when I was really little I wanted to be the Queen.
FIGURE 6: Yeah, like that's going to happen.
FIGURE 5: I wanted to be the Queen of Australia.
FARRAH: And that's good because you were just thinking big. And so what if that changes and so what if it seems impossible? Why shouldn't you have big dreams and bold dreams no matter where you come from? What says to you you have to do what's expected or only reach as far as you think you can? There's plenty of time to be realistic and to compromise.
FIGURE 2: Farrah's right.
FIGURE 3: Yeah, that's really it, Farrah.
FIGURE 4: Nice one, dude.

FIGURE 5: Word up, captain.
FARRAH: Shut up.
FIGURE 6: Or she'll put us all in the brig.
FIGURE 2: Or she'll throw us overboard.
FARRAH: Yeah.

The FIGURES *exit.*

JACK: So what are we going to do?

Pause.

FARRAH: Spec.
JACK: [*with a laugh*] Yeah?
FARRAH: Speculate about where to from here.
JACK: A swim at Nobbys?
FARRAH: Nah.
JACK: A trip to Sydney.
FARRAH: Okay.
JACK: The boat museum in Darling Harbour.
FARRAH: Maybe.
JACK: Lunch at the overseas terminal.
FARRAH: And that's your shout, is it?
JACK: Shout!
FARRAH: Is there an eight-storey cruise ship in the dock?
JACK: The *Queen Mary*.
FARRAH: Yeah.
JACK: Speed back up the highway.
FARRAH: Within the speed limit.
JACK: That too.
FARRAH: Yeah.
JACK: All good.
FARRAH: Yeah.
JACK: Yeah.

Pause.

FARRAH: Spec, shout, speed. So where's the sock?

He waits, then leans in to kiss her.

Sock.
JACK: And if you want the spill you'll have to read my blog.

FARRAH: What?
JACK: shipping enthusiast.com
FARRAH: It is not.
JACK: Check it out.

He flicks her with something as he exits. She flicks him back.

SCENE TWENTY-ONE

One of the MATILDAS *emerges as a single mother figure. She is with* FARRAH.

MATILDA: It's my way of saying that I'm sorry.
FARRAH: I know.
MATILDA: I didn't believe you when you said that you didn't do the graffiti.
FARRAH: I know.
MATILDA: I didn't even really listen to you properly.
FARRAH: I know.
MATILDA: I'm always busy and I'm always late.
FARRAH: I know.
MATILDA: So this is my way of saying that I'm sorry. Coming out here to look at it.
FARRAH: West Basin.
MATILDA: What's that?
FARRAH: That's the berth, it's called West Basin.

Pause.

MATILDA: I've never understood what you see in them.
FARRAH: I know.
MATILDA: All these years, I've never realised that you were serious.
FARRAH: I know.
MATILDA: But it's a new day.
FARRAH: It is.
MATILDA: If you want to go into all of this as a career. Well, I won't stop you.
FARRAH: I know.
MATILDA: Stop saying I know.
FARRAH: But I do know.

MATILDA: Do you? I wish I had your confidence in me as a mother. I think I've been rubbish at it.
FARRAH: You have.
MATILDA: What?
FARRAH: And I'd like you to have your replacement in place before you leave.
MATILDA: What?
FARRAH: I'm firing you.
MATILDA: Firing me?
FARRAH: That's right.
MATILDA: You can't fire someone from being your mother.
FARRAH: Exactly. So you just get on with it.

> *Pause.*

MATILDA: Would you want to?
FARRAH: Fire you?
MATILDA: If you could?
FARRAH: Sure.
MATILDA: That's not what you're supposed to say.
FARRAH: Mum.
MATILDA: You're supposed to say you understand. You understand that I've had to work day and night to give you what I can. That I've got caught up in that and if, sometimes, I've left you too long to your own devices well, I can make it up to you now.
FARRAH: You've brought me out to see the *Pasha Bulker* in berth, haven't you?
MATILDA: What do you think they'll do with it now?
FARRAH: The papers are saying that it will be taken to Brisbane for repairs and then I imagine if it's still seaworthy they'll give it a new name.
MATILDA: But it's famous as the *Pasha Bulker*.
FARRAH: It's famous for being grounded.
MATILDA: Good point.

> *Pause.*

FARRAH: The harbourmaster has invited me to accompany him on a piloting operation. Can I go?
MATILDA: What is it?

FARRAH: You get helicoptered out to a bulk carrier off the coast then you move rapidly but carefully across the deck up into the bridge of the ship and observe as the marine pilot navigates the vessel into one of the Kooragang berths.

MATILDA: And if I say no you probably really will fire me as your mother?

FARRAH: Yep.

MATILDA: And that's what you'd be doing if you wanted to take this up as a job?

FARRAH: Oh no, mostly I'd be doing cutter transfers which involves you climbing about nine metres up a ladder on the side of a moving ship. If they privatise the ports probably more and more of them will be cutter transfers.

MATILDA: I'm sorry I asked.

FARRAH: You get training, Mum. In Tasmania. There's even a simulator.

MATILDA: It's such a big responsibility.

FARRAH: And isn't that what Nanna said to you when you decided to have me as a single parent?

Pause.

MATILDA: She couldn't stop me. I'd never been so elated, terrified and nervous about anything I'd ever done.

FARRAH: But that's no reason not to do it.

MATILDA: Well, that doesn't sound like someone who's grounded anymore.

FARRAH: Blame it on the *Pasha Bulker*.

MATILDA: I beg your pardon?

FARRAH: There's a song.

MATILDA: And if you sing it, the answer will definitely be no.

FARRAH: I'm not going to sing.

MATILDA: Then… yes.

FARRAH *makes the sound of the tug whistle.*

Do it again.

The full cast make the sound of the tug whistle.

THE END

www.ingramcontent.com/pod-product-compliance
Lightning Source LLC
Chambersburg PA
CBHW042130160426
43198CB00022B/2967